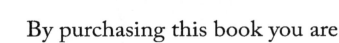

ISBN 978-0-666-11982-7
PIBN 10602770

This book is a reproduction of an important historical work. Forgotten Books uses state-of-the-art technology to digitally reconstruct the work, preserving the original format whilst repairing imperfections present in the aged copy. In rare cases, an imperfection in the original, such as a blemish or missing page, may be replicated in our edition. We do, however, repair the vast majority of imperfections successfully; any imperfections that remain are intentionally left to preserve the state of such historical works.

THE UNITED STATES
STRATEGIC BOMBING SURVEY

Reports Pacific war 7

KAWANISHI AIRCRAFT CO.
(Kawanishi Kokuki Kabushiki Kaisha)

CORPORATION REPORT No. III
(Air frames)

D7 5. Ues

No 18-22

6

AIRCRAFT DIVISION

April 1947

1676

THE UNITED STATES
STRATEGIC BOMBING SURVEY

Report. Pacific war no. 21

SUMITOMO METAL INDUSTRIES, PROPELLER DIVISION

(SUMITOMO KINZOKU KOGYO K K, PUROPERA SEIZOSHO)

CORPORATION REPORT No. VI
(PROPELLORS)

December 1946

THE UNITED STATES
STRATEGIC BOMBING SURVEY

SUMITOMO METAL INDUSTRIES, PROPELLER DIVISION

(SUMITOMO KINZOKU KOGYO K K, PUROPERA SEIZOSHO)

CORPORATION REPORT No. VI
(PROPELLORS)

Dates of Survey:

20 October 1945—28 October 1945

December 1946

This report was written primarily for the use of the United States Strategic Bombing Survey in the preparation of further reports of a more comprehensive nature. Any conclusions or opinions expressed in this report must be considered as limited to the specific material covered and as subject to further interpretation in the light of further studies conducted by the Survey.

FOREWORD

The United States Strategic Bombing Survey was established by the Secretary of War on 3 November 1944, pursuant to a directive from the late President Roosevelt. Its mission was to conduct an impartial and expert study of the effects of our aerial attack on Germany, to be used in connection with air attacks on Japan and to establish a basis for evaluating the importance and potentialities of air power as an instrument of military strategy for planning the future development of the United States armed forces and for determining future economic policies with respect to the national defense. A summary report and some 200 supporting reports containing the findings of the Survey in Germany have been published.

On 15 August 1945, President Truman requested that the Survey conduct a similar study of the effects of all types of air attack in the war against Japan, submitting reports in duplicate to the Secretary of War and to the Secretary of the Navy. The officers of the Survey during its Japanese phase were:

Franklin D'Olier, *Chairman*.
Paul H. Nitze, Henry C. Alexander, *Vice-Chairmen*.
Harry L. Bowman,
J. Kenneth Galbraith,
Rensis Likert,
Frank A. McNamee, Jr.,
Fred Searls, Jr.,
Monroe E. Spaght,
Dr. Lewis R. Thompson,
Theodore P. Wright, *Directors*.
Walter Wilds, *Secretary*.

The Survey's complement provided for 300 civilians, 350 officers, and 500 enlisted men. The military segment of the organization was drawn from the Army to the extent of 60 percent, and from the Navy to the extent of 40 percent. Both the Army and the Navy gave the Survey all possible assistance in furnishing men, supplies, transport, and information. The Survey operated from headquarters established in Tokyo early in September 1945, with subheadquarters in Nagoya, Osaka, Hiroshima, and Nagasaki, and with mobile teams operating in other parts of Japan, the islands of the Pacific, and the Asiatic mainland.

It was possible to reconstruct much of wartime Japanese military planning and execution, engagement by engagement, and campaign by campaign, and to secure reasonably accurate statistics on Japan's economy and war production, plant by plant, and industry by industry. In addition, studies were conducted on Japan's over-all strategic plans and the background of her entry into the war, the internal discussions and negotiations leading to her acceptance of unconditional surrender, the course of health and morale among the civilian population, the effectiveness of the Japanese civilian defense organization, and the effects of the atomic bombs. Separate reports will be issued covering each phase of the study.

The Survey interrogated more than 700 Japanese military, government, and industrial officials. It also recovered and translated many documents which not only have been useful to the Survey, but also will furnish data valuable for other studies. Arrangements have been made to turn over the Survey's files to the Central Intelligence Group, through which they will be available for further examination and distribution.

TABLE OF CONTENTS

Introduction

The leading manufacturer of propellers in the Japanese Empire, the Sumitomo Propeller Division (Sumitomo Puropera Seizosho) of the Sumitomo Metal Industries (Sumitomo Kinzoku Kogyo K K), produced 66 percent of all propellers used in Japanese aircraft. This represented practically all the propellers for the Japanese Navy, and nearly 40 percent of the propellers used by Army aircraft. The Sumitomo Corporation concentrated on the reduction of two main types of propellers, the

Hamilton standard counterweight type and the Vereinigte Deutsche Metallwerke (VDM) type. Being financially strong, well organized, and by using production line techniques (by Japanese standards) the propeller division delivered 3,140 propellers in July 1944 when peak production was reached.

Sumitomo began the production of metal alloy propellers in March 1933 at their copper works located in Sakurajima, north of Osaka Harbor (Figure 1): In October 1935 the demand for variable pitch propellers prompted Sumitomo to pur-

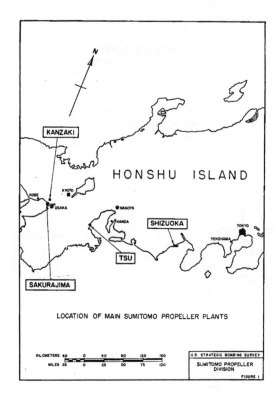

KANZAKI

HONSHU ISLAND

KOBE
KYOTO
OSAKA
NAGOYA
HANDA
SHIZUOKA
TOKYO
YOKOHAMA
TSU

SAKURAJIMA

LOCATION OF MAIN SUMITOMO PROPELLER PLANTS

| KILOMETERS | 40 | 0 | 40 | 80 | 120 | 160 |
| MILES | 25 | 0 | 25 | 50 | 75 | 100 |

U.S STRATEGIC BOMBING SURVEY

SUMITOMO PROPELLER DIVISION

FIGURE 1

clase the patents of the VDM type from Germany, while the patents for the Hamilton type were purchased through the American Government. By 1937 manufacture of propellers had increased to such proportions that officials of the Sumitomo Metals Industry placed Sakurajima on a divisional status on equal standing with the corporation's other divisions. In November the copper works at Sakurajima was divided into two parts, the Copper Works and the Propeller Works.

The possibility production requirements would become greater than the capacity of the Sakurajima plant was quickly recognized by the officials of the Sumitomo Propeller Division. In January 1939 a new site was purchased at Kanzaki, 1 mile north of Amagasaki and about 5 miles northwest of Osaka. Construction of the Kanzaki plant was completed early in 1941 and in April of that year initial production began. Concurrently with the

establishment of this new plant, the offices o propeller division were moved from Sakurajin the new location and were maintained there administrative purposes. At the same time search and design section, charged with the c opment of prototype propellers, was establish Kanzaki.

The outbreak of World War II and the s quent increase in demands from both the Navy Army resulted in the establishment of two propeller plants at Shizuoka and Tsu. The S oka plant, located in Shizuoka prefecture just of the city of Shizuoka, was completed and menced production in March 1943. The Tsu to the south of the city of Tsu, was converted already existing buildings of a cotton mill began propeller production in September 194

The propeller division, one of six divisions c Sumitomo Metal Industries (Figure 2), was f

SUBSIDIARY WORKS
SUMITOMO METAL INDUSTRY

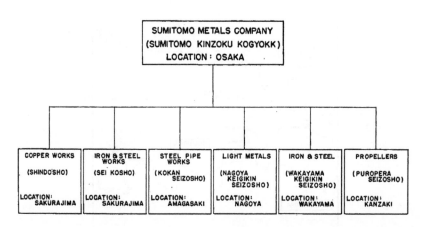

FIGURE

cially dependent upon the parent company. Similarly, the Sumitomo corporation was dependent upon the Sumitomo Trust for financial support.

The Kanzaki Plant made both the Hamilton counterweight propellers and the VDM type, but the three subordinate plants, Sakurajima, Tsu, and

Shizuoka, produced the Hamilton type only pendix A). Due to the abrupt ending of th the three smaller plants never reached the intended for them as equals to the Kanzaki Each plant produced its own blade and hub blies and did the final assembly of the fi

ict. Had the war continued it was planned to te VDM production in the three smaller plants his had been prohibitive through August 1945 o the retooling required, the great increase in assembly time, and the consequent drop in all propeller production.

cause Sumitomo was the acknowledged leader e propeller field and employed some of the ng Japanese research engineers there was conible pressure from the government agencies umitomo, particularly in the field of new ns.

:eet supervision by the Navy or Army was applied and no military personnel were stai at any plant in other than routine resident ctor status. Both branches of the service were y interested in developing a "full-feathering" lton type propeller, favoring the Hamilton over VDM. However, since the VDM type !ull-feathering and Sumitomo engineers were successful in obtaining a blade angle greater 60° on the Hamilton, the emphasis was on the type at the close of the war despite producdifficulties. Similarly, both the Army and

Navy were interested in hollow steel blades and counter-rotating six-bladed propellers capable of absorbing the high horsepower of some of the new experimental engines.

Financial aid from state banks was never requested since the propeller division always applied to the Sumitomo Metals Industries for any financial help.

Organization and Operation

Since Kanzaki was the largest plant of the division the chief of the Kanzaki plant, Osamu Sugimoto, was also president of the Sumitomo Propeller Division. An exceedingly able man, having studied in the graduate school of aeronautics at Massachusetts Institute of Technology, Sugimoto was also titular head of Sumitomo's research and design section. Assisting the president as production chief and executive vice president respectively were Bunzo Hito and Isamu Shirai. The remaining three men on the staff of the Sumitomo Propeller Division were as follows: Soji Hori, chief of the Sakurajima plant, Joyoei Takesako, chief of the Shizuoka plant, and Michitoshi Kitano, the chief of the Tsu plant (Figure 3).

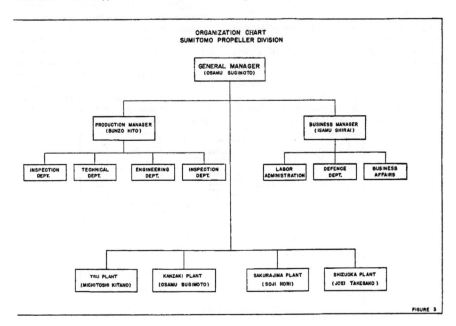

ORGANIZATION CHART
SUMITOMO PROPELLER DIVISION

FIGURE 3

3

Production methods of the division (Appendices B and C) were considered excellent when judged by Japanese standards, but the plants were without the modern mass production equipment employed by leading American manufacturers. There were no mechanical conveyor systems and, although original contour cuts were made by machine, complete hand grinding was necessary in the blade finishing section. The number of vehicles available for transportation of parts between buildings was negligible.

A system of confining workers to a single specialized job was successful, and it is perhaps significant to note that increases in production were sometimes accompanied by a decrease in man-hours, indicating the skill of individual workers at particular jobs had greatly improved. "Job shop" practices were not employed in any plant and even the various dispersed locations maintained assembly-line techniques. The relatively high efficiency of the Sumitomo plant was attributed to the fact that many of its officials had visited the United States, and Sugimoto had personally visited the Hamilton Standard Propeller Division of United Aircraft in Hartford, Conn.

Employment

Beginning in 1933, when the first propellers were produced at the Sakurajima plant, the Sumitomo Propeller Division always used a two-shift system. The day shift, utilizing about 85 percent of the employees, began work at 0730 and worked through 0730 that evening. Although the night shift was considered a production shift, only the machining sections functioned. All subassembly and final assembly shops were closed down. Officials of the company never considered establishing a third shift working day because of the problems it would create. A great increase in labor would have been necessary and an additional burden placed on the already overloaded public transportation system.

Although labor trouble was never considered a "bottleneck," examination of daily work attendance records reveals a surprisingly high percentage of absenteeism at all plants. The over-all absenteeism at the Sumitomo plants appeared to be about to 15 percent. Officials at Sumitomo were requested to explain why the Japanese government would allow such high absenteeism in such an important part of the war industry. Their explanation was that the government would not allow them to drop workers from the plant rolls even though some of them had been ill for many months. Thus, in many cases, people were carried on the rolls of Sumitomo who were not and had not been productive labor for extremely long periods.

Officials were questioned as to whether or not the Sumitomo company paid these individuals and it was discovered that when an individual worker was absent for a period exceeding 14 days he was no longer paid by the company but was given unemployment compensation by the Japanese government. When Sumitomo was required to submit figures to the Government relative to absenteeism they therefore prepared three percentages for each month; one, the total figure; two, the percent absent which normally would be dropped from rolls; and three, the actual absentee figure.

Peak employment was reached in November 1 when 23,160 employees were working at the four plants (Figure 4).

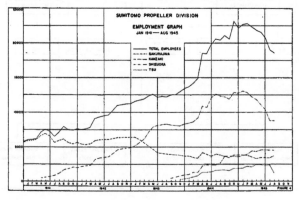

times, the projected movements could have been speeded up by several months and probably completed by late summer.

Like other aircraft companies, Sumitomo favored dispersing plants to ex-schools and converted mills (Figure 5). Kanzaki, for example, dispersed to Kainan, a converted weaving mill; Naniwa, Sanda, Saijo, and Ikedo, all converted school buildings; and Hirono, a newly constructed, semiunderground, factory built by Sumitomo at Hirono village.

Since in most cases the dispersed sites were in the same general area as the parent plant (Appendix D) no major labor trouble was experienced. Many families had already moved from industrial sections into suburban areas near dispersed plant sites and some further movement of Sumitomo employees was undertaken as part of the general dispersal program. Sumitomo officials expected labor conditions to be better after dispersal because there would be fewer man-hour losses caused by alerts. The mental state of individual workers, released from the strain of constant bombings, was also expected to improve.

It was estimated by officials of the corporation that problems connected with dispersal alone, disregarding any other wartime difficulties, would have caused production at the various plants to drop until August 1945, after which, it was hoped, recuperation would begin. Kanzaki plant management estimated their production would drop to 30 percent, and Tsu, 60 percent.

THE AIR ATTACKS

Heavily damaged by area attacks against major cities, or attacked directly as assigned targets, all four of the main Sumitomo plants suffered from the B-29 raids during the period of 1 June until 26 June 1945. Both Kanzaki and Sakurajima, the two larger plants, were destroyed almost completely—production at Kanzaki dropping from 1,672 propellers in May to 377 in June, and at Sakurajima from 1,016 in May to 100 in June.

Never a target for direct attack, the Kanzaki plant was nevertheless heavily damaged and lost 90 percent of its productive capacity in the area attack against Amagasaki on 15 June 1945. In the area attack of 1 June 40 incendiary bombs landed within the plant area but were quickly extinguished by the air raid defense corps without damage to the plant. No extensive repair of damaged buildings or heavy equipment was undertaken at Kanzaki after the 15 June raid but it was planned to attempt

SUMITOMO PROPELLER DIVISION
PLANNED VS. COMPLETED DISPERSAL

FIGURE 5

PARENT PLANT	DISPERSAL	TYPE	FLOOR AREA SQ.FT.	PRODUCTS	NO. OF MACHINE TOOLS		NO. OF WORKERS		DATE OF BEGINNING PRODUCTION	PERCENTAGE OF COMPLETION	REMARKS
					PLAN	ACTUAL	PLAN	ACTUAL			
KANZAKI	KAINAN	SPINNING MILL	74,595	HUBS FOR VDM TYPE	85	83	500	300	FEB. 1945	100%	
	SHIJO	SCHOOL	21,528	JIGS & TOOLS	50	49	200	4	MAR. 1945	100%	
	NANIWA	SCHOOL	27,986	RESEARCH & DESIGN	10	10	100	100	FEB. 1945	100%	
	IKEDA	SCHOOL	17,222	JIGS & TOOLS	0	0	21	21	FEB. 1945	100%	
	HIRONO	FOREST PLANT / TUNNEL	150,696 / 48,438	ASSEMBLY, VDM TYPE	515	334	4000	500	NOT OPERATING	30%	
	SANDA	SCHOOL	32,292	ASSEMBLY OF PITCH CONTROLLING PARTS FOR VDM TYPE PROPELLER	15	10	210	210	MAR. 1945	100%	FRONT SLIDE GEAR REAR SLIDE GEAR & REAR COVERS FOR FRONT GEAR CASES
SAKURAJIMA	SOGO	DEPARTMENT STORE BASEMENT	240,026	LARGE PARTS OF HAMILTON TYPE PROPELLER	143	143	1060	1019	JUNE 1945	100%	SPIDERS, HUBS, PISTONS & CYLINDERS
	MATSUZAKAYA	DEPARTMENT STORE BASEMENT	69,438	MEDIUM & SMALL PARTS OF HAMILTON TYPE PROPELLER	247	247	1600	116	JUNE 1945	100%	BLADE BUSHINGS SPINNER BOLTS, PISTONS, GASKETS & NUTS
	NISHINOMIYA	UNION BEER BREWERY	253,202	FINAL ASSEMBLY & BLADE MACHINING 'H' TYPE	111	111	1100	1076	JULY 1945	90%	
SHIZUOKA	HATORI	FOREST PLANT	62,969	MACHINING PARTS OF 'H' TYPE	360	181	2500	767	MAY 1945	40%	SPIDERS, HUBS, PISTON, CYLINDERS, BUSHINGS, GASKETS, NUTS & ETC.
TSU	HANDA	TUNNEL	61,355	MACHINING PARTS OF 'H' AND VDM TYPE PROPS	640	271	4500	725	MAY 1945	70%	H { SPIDERS, CYLINDERS, HUBS, BUSHINGS & PISTONS VDM { BLADE SUPPORTER, FIRST & SECOND SLIDE GEARS, HUBS & WING ROTATING GEARS

pair of enough of the superficially damaged machinery to permit production of 350 Hamilton type propellers monthly—20 percent of the May production. Undamaged machinery was dispersed to the Girono, Shizuoka and Tsu plants.

Two air attacks directly affected production at the Sakurajima plant. The first occurred on 1 June 1945 and the second on 24 July 1945. Damage from the former attack was slight, only a few incendiary bombs falling within the plant compound; the second attack, however, completely wrecked the plant. Since dispersal had already been accomplished, the attack of 24 July did not affect production to any great extent and it was planned to continue production at Nishinomiya, Ogo, and Matsuzakaya. Although Nishinomiya was damaged considerably in the area attack of 6 August, recovery was rapid and it was hoped that production would be regained by 1 September.

The Tsu plant was damaged only slightly in the attack of 26 June. A considerable part of the dispersal to Handa had, however, already been completed. It was planned to produce approximately 00 Hamilton and 500 VDM type propellers month-

ly at Handa by December 1945. The original Tsu plant was to be retained as a warehouse for parts and material only.

The Shizuoka plant, as a result of the air attacks of 20 June, lost 99 percent of its productive capacity. Complete recuperation was not considered possible but it was planned to continue limited assembly work at the undamaged shops until the Hatori plant was completed and could attain a production rate of approximately 500 Hamilton type propellers monthly—expected by December 1945.

PRODUCTION STATISTICS

The period of greatest production for the Sumitomo Propeller Division was from April 1944 through March 1945. During that period 32,596 propellers were produced, representing 72 percent of government short-range orders and 77 percent of capacity (Appendix E).

The Kanzaki plant was the largest producer, manufacturing approximately 50 percent of all the Sumitomo propellers. Production from the Sakurajima plant increased until June 1945 when it produced approximately 53 percent of total production (Figure 6). Production of both Tsu and Shizu-

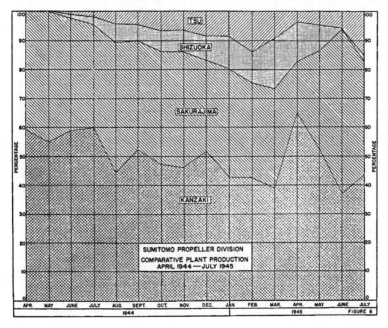

SUMITOMO PROPELLER DIVISION
COMPARATIVE PLANT PRODUCTION
APRIL 1944—JULY 1945

FIGURE 6

7

oka also increased until March 1945 when they contributed about 27 percent of the total. Capacity production was never attained, but during July 1944 a total of 3,140 propellers was produced representing 79 percent of estimated capacity. From December 1944 until the close of the war, peak capacity and actual production declined sharply due to air attacks and problems connected with dispersal (Appendix F).

In the first half year of 1945 alerts and actual raids caused a lowering of production capabilities. Officials of the company estimated that losses due to alerts and air raids were 10 percent at all pla[ ]Engineers at the Kanzaki plant also claimed t[ ]potential capacity was greatly reduced beca[ ]they were forced to make the VDM type prope[ ]which required approximately 75 percent more [ ]assembly time.

The officials of Sumitomo believed that the g[ ]ernment planned production for the corporat[ ]was too high through March 1945, but thereaf[ ]had the propeller division of Sumitomo maintai[ ]ns war time rate of expansion (Figure 7), qu[ ]

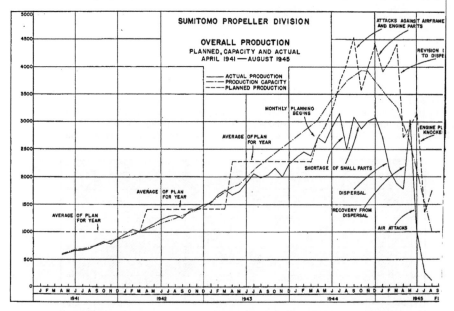

SUMITOMO PROPELLER DIVISION

OVERALL PRODUCTION
PLANNED, CAPACITY AND ACTUAL
APRIL 1941 — AUGUST 1945

would have been attainable. Government orders were submitted in October for the ensuing year and long-range planning was accomplished at this time. Short-range planning was based on quarterly production figures submitted approximately two months before the beginning of a new quarter.

The over-all production of the Sumitomo Propeller Division is shown in Figure 7. Unusual fluctuations in production are explained on the graph, but it may be significant to point out that although government orders do not include requests for wooden-bladed propellers, the actual production included approximately 400 such propellers. Forced to conserve aluminum, Sumitomo began the[ ]duction of the wooden-bladed Hamilton typ[ ]January 1945 and had produced 120 during[ ]month of June.

According to production leads of the com[ ]failure on the part of Sumitomo to meet Go[ ]ment orders was attributed to various causes.[ ]lack of raw materials, or, more correctly, the[ ]control over raw materials by the governmen[ ]considered the chief "bottleneck" (Reference[ ]1). In many instances materials contracte[ ]were not received on time, thus making fulfill[ ]of committments an impossibility. In the op[ ]

8

EVALUATION OF PREATTACK
INTELLIGENCE

Sufficient data was not available for WD Military Intelligence Service G-2 to predict montly production of propellers. However, quarterly estimates, made up through the first quarter of 1944, were generally correct though slightly low. Intelligence sources did not reveal the fact that the Tsu plant was in operation and no mention was made in Military Intelligence Service reports to the production of this plant.

REFERENCE ITEMS

The following material is in the files of USSBS, Aircraft Division, in the Office of the Adjutant General, War Department, Washington, D. C.

REFERENCE ITEM 1. Chart, "Raw Materials Received Compared With Amount Ordered or Contracted For." Sumitomo Corporation Report No. VI.

APPENDIX A
SUMITOMO PROPELLER DIVISION PRODUCTS

Blade Size	Shank Size	Type	Aircraft	Manufactured By—	For—	Shipped to—	Br S
A	D	H	A6M2 (Zeke 21)	Sakurajima	Mitsubishi	Nagoya	
AB	D	H	A6M2-K (Zeke trainer)	Sakurajima	Hitachi	Chiba	
					Nakajima	Koizumi	
C	D	H	A6A15 (Zeke 52)	Sakurajima	Mitsubishi	Nagoya	
					Mitsubishi	Suzuka	
					Nakajima	Koizumi	
					Hitachi	Chiba	
D	D	H	Q1W1 (Lorna)	Sakurajima	Kyushy-Hikoki		
E	E	H	E13A1 (Jake II)	Kanzaki	Aichi	Nagoya	
				Sakurajima	Aichi	Nagoya	
F	E	H	L2D3 (Tabby 22)	Kanzaki	Showa-Hikoki		
				Sakurajima	Showa Hikoki		
	E	H	P1Y1 (Frances II)	Kanzaki	Nakajima	Koizumi	
				Shizuoka	Nakajima	Koizumi	
H	E	H	P1Y1-S (Frances II)	Kanzaki	Kawanishi	Konan	
H	E	H	P1Y1 (Frances)	Kanzaki	Kawanishi	Konan	
I	E	H	D4Y1 (Judy II)	Kanzaki	Aichi	Nagoya	
				Shizuoka	Aichi	Nagoya	
I	E	H	D4Y2 (Judy 12)	Kanzaki	Aichi	Nagoya	
				Shizuoka	Aichi	Nagoya	
J	E	H	D4A1 (exp. Judy)	Kanzaki	Aichi	Nagoya	
				Shizuoka	Aichi	Nagoya	
K	E	H	M6A1 (Seiran)	Kanzaki	Aichi	Nagoya	
G	E	H	C6N1 (Myrt II)	Kanzaki	Nakajima	Koizumi	
				Shizuoka	Nakajima	Koizumi	
				Kanzaki	Nakajima	Handa	
				Shizuoka	Nakajima	Handa	
H	E		B6N2 (Jill 12)	Kanzaki	Nakajima	Handa	
L	E		K8K2 (Emily 12)	Kanzaki	Kawanishi	Konan	
H	E		G4M2 (Betty 22)	Kanzaki	Mitsubishi	Nagoya	
H	E	H	G4M2-A (Betty 24)	Kanzaki	Mitsubishi	Nagoya	
				Kanznki	Mitsubishi	Mizushima	
H	E	H	G4M3 (Betty 34)	Kanzaki	Mitsubishi	Nagoya	
				Kanzaki	Mitsubishi	Mizushima	
M	E	H	J2M3 (Jack 21)	Kanzaki	Mitsubishi	Nagoya	
				Kanzaki	Mitsubishi	Suzuka	
				Kanzaki		Koza	
N	E	VDM	N1K1-J (George)	Kanzaki	Kawanishi	Naruo	
				Kanzaki	Kawanishi	Himeji	
O	E	VDM	B7A1 (Grace II)	Kanzaki	Aichi	Nagoya	
P	E	VDM	J5N1 (Tenrai)	Kanzaki	Nakajima	Koizumi	
Q	E	H	E16A1 (Paul II)	Kanzaki	Aichi	Nagoya	
				Kanzaki	Nippon-Hikoki		
R	E	H	D3A1 (Val 22)	Kanzaki	Aichi	Nagoya	
				Sakurajima	Aichi	Nagoya	
S	E	VDM	A7M1 (Sam II)	Kanzaki	Mitsubishi	Nagoya	
T	E	H	D4Y3 (Judy 33)	Kanzaki	Aichi	Nagoya	
				Shizuoka	Aichi	Nagoya	
				Tsu	Aichi	Nagoya	
M	E	VDM	J2M4 (Jack)	Kanzaki	Mitsubishi	Suzuka	
				Kanzaki		Koza	
N	E	VDM	N1K2-J (George 21)	Kanzaki	Mitsubishi	Mizushima	
				Kanzaki	Aichi	Nagoya	
				Kanzaki	Kawanishi	Naruo	
				Kanzaki	Kawanishi	Himeji	
				Kanzaki	Showa-Hikoki		
				Kanzaki		Koza	
Exp.	E	H	D3Y1 (Exp. Val)				
M	E	VDM	J2M5 (Jack)	Kanzaki	Mitsubishi	Nagoya	
				Kanzaki	Mitsubishi	Suzuka	
U	E	VDM	Ki-67 (Peggy)	Kanzaki		Kagamigahara	
V	E	VDM	Ki-74 (Patsy)	Kanzaki		Tachikawa	
W	E	VDM	Ki-83	Kanzaki		Kagamigahara	
X	E	H	Ki-51 (Sonia 1)	Sakurajima		Tachikawa	
Y	E	H	Ki-46 IV (Dinah 4)	Tsu		Kagamigahara	
T	E	H	Ki-61 II (Tony 2)	Tsu		Kagamigahara	
X	E	H	Ki-105	Sakurajima		Osaka	
Y	E	H	Ki-100	Tsu		Kagamigahara	

NOTES
1. Columns 1 and 2 indicate the various blade-and-shank size combinations used on different aircraft as shown in Column 4.
2. Column 3. H—Hamilton type counterweight propeller. VDM—Vereinigte Deutsche Metallwerke type.
All Army propellers were shipped to Army depots, not direct to manufacturers.

10

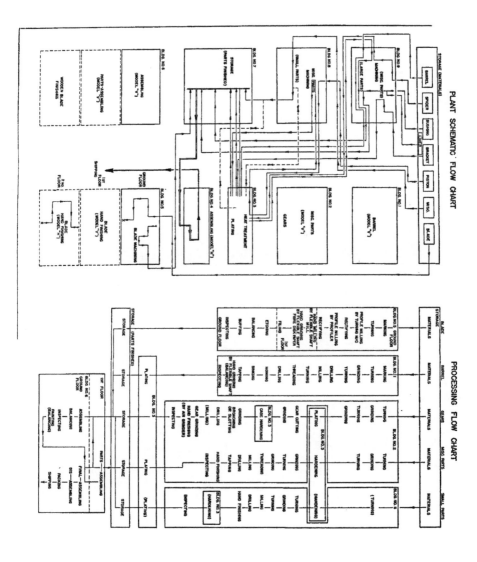

FLOW CHART

HAMILTON TYPE PROPELLER

FLOW CHART
VDM TYPE PROPELLER

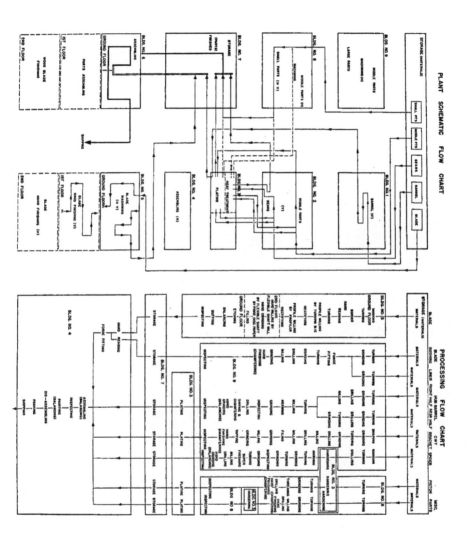

PLANT SCHEMATIC FLOW CHART

PROCESSING FLOW CHART

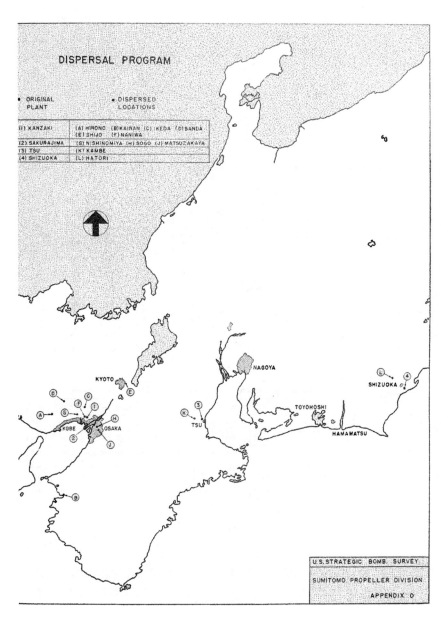

DISPERSAL PROGRAM

● ORIGINAL   ● DISPERSED
  PLANT   LOCATIONS

(1) KANZAKI	(A) HIRONO (B) KAINAN (C) IKEDA (D) SANDA
	(E) SHIJO (F) NANIWA
(2) SAKURAJIMA	(G) NISHINOMIYA (H) SOGO (J) MATSUZAKAYA
(3) TSU	(K) KAMBE
(4) SHIZUOKA	(L) HATORI

U.S. STRATEGIC BOMB. SURVEY

SUMITOMO PROPELLER DIVISION

APPENDIX D

11

APPENDIX E
PLANNED, CAPACITY, AND ACTUAL PRODUCTION BY MONTHS
SUMITOMO PROPELLER DIVISION

Period	Production capacity, H-type Propeller								1941	
	1933	1934	1935	1936	1937	1938	1939	1940	H Capacity	H
January..........................	....	20	39	58	110	230	340	460	570	....
February.........................	....	22	40	60	120	235	350	470	580	....
March............................	....	24	41	61	130	200	360	479	590	....
Total Fiscal..............	....	166	407	626	1,026	2,330	3,660	5,099	6,449	....
April.............................	....	26	43	62	140	250	370	488	600	
May..............................	....	28	45	63	160	260	380	497	632	
June.............................	10	29	47	65	170	270	390	506	684	
July.............................	11	30	49	67	180	280	400	515	696	
August...........................	13	31	50	69	190	290	410	573	728	
September........................	14	33	51	70	195	300	420	530	760	
October..........................	16	35	52	80	200	310	430	540	802	
November.........................	17	37	54	90	210	320	440	550	835	
December.........................	19	38	55	100	220	330	450	560	883	
Total Year..............	100	353	567	845	2,025	3,275	4,740	6,168	8,337	

Period	1942				1943			
	Capacity		Actual		Capacity		Actual	
	H	VDM	H	VDM	H	VDM	H	V
January.........................	910	0	974	0	1,425	122	1,526	
February........................	947	10	1,050	0	1,510	133	1,684	
March...........................	990	20	1,005	0	1,585	145	1,755	
Total fiscal..............	11,184	30	9,501	0	15,049	1,030	16,572	
April...........................	1,027	30	1,088	0	1,655	157	1,666	
May.............................	1,065	40	1,150	0	1,700	168	1,725	
June............................	1,102	50	1,234	0	1,825	170	1,883	
July............................	1,140	60	1,277	0	1,940	185	2,006	
August..........................	1,180	70	1,302	0	2,020	200	1,930	
September.......................	1,120	80	1,253	0	2,102	220	1,973	
October.........................	1,255	90	1,375	0	2,186	240	2,109	
November........................	1,300	100	1,427	0	2,270	255	1,948	
December........................	1,340	110	1,501	0	2,352	275	2,175	
Total year..............	13,376	660	14,636	0	22,570	2,270	22,380	

Period	1944										
	Planned		Capacity		Actual		Planned		Capacity		
	H	VDM	H	VDM	H	VDM	H	VDM	H	VDM	H
January..........................	....	....	2,432	290	2,292	63	2,792	915	3,053	530	2,360
February.........................	....	....	2,516	310	2,377	71	3,023	1,095	2,882	543	1,888
March............................	....	....	2,598	330	2,283	92	3,200	1,230	2,710	560	1,780
Total Fiscal..............	....	....	25,606	2,800	24,367	575	35,170	10,197	37,220	5,503	28,593
April............................	2,350	350	2,680	350	2,461	253	2,120	600	2,355	580	1,280
May..............................	2,450	450	2,860	370	2,371	250	2,175	760	2,010	600	2,370
June.............................	2,640	570	3,015	390	2,493	404	2,230	910	1,611	470	699
July.............................	2,875	825	3,175	410	2,684	456	1,940	150	1,212	340	185
August...........................	3,025	1,030	3,320	430	2,187	305	1,450	300	800	200	50
September........................	3,310	1,230	3,395	450	2,614	458	1,580	450	....	....	....
October..........................	2,901	687	3,470	470	2,649	220	.....¹	....	....	....	....
November.........................	3,197	830	3,430	490	2,609	401	....	....	....	....	....
December.........................	3,407	995	3,230	510	2,497	576	....	....	....	....	....
	26,155	6,967	36,121	4,800	29,517	3,549	¹18,190	¹ 5,950	16,633	3,823	10,612

¹ To August.

NOTE 1.—Monthly planning did not begin until April, 1944. Long-range plans for the fiscal year (April–March) started in 1939–40 (7,350 prop types), continuing with 9,000 propellers for 1940 41, 12,000 for 1941 to 1945, and 30,000 H-type and 20,000 VDM-type for the year April 1945 to 1946.

NOTE 2.—Grand totals for production capacity, commencing April 1941, were 97,047 H-type propellers and 11,553 VDM-type propellers, and f production were 83,707 H-type propellers and 6,178 VDM-type propellers. The grand total for planned production April 1941–March 1946 was 158 as much as 113,705 referred to H-type propellers. Types were not separated in planning until 1943–44.

12

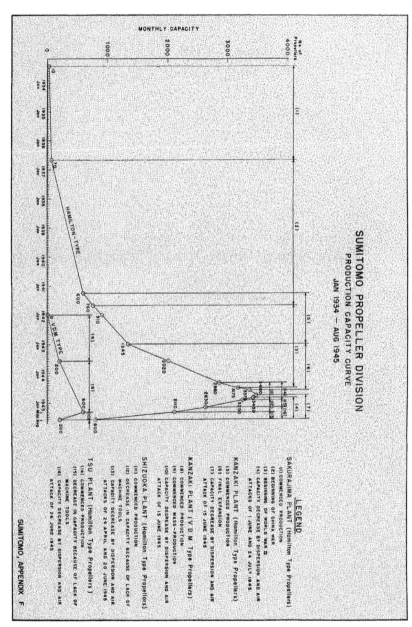

SUMITOMO PROPELLER DIVISION
PRODUCTION CAPACITY CURVE
JAN 1934 — AUG 1945

MONTHLY CAPACITY

No. of Propellers
4000
3000
2000
1000
0

HAMILTON-TYPE

V.D.M. TYPE

LEGEND

SAKURAJIMA PLANT (Hamilton Type Propellers)
(1) COMMENCED PRODUCTION
(2) BEGINNING OF CHINA WAR
(3) BEGINNING OF WORLD WAR II
(4) CAPACITY DECREASE BY DISPERSION AND AIR
    ATTACK OF 1 JUNE AND 24 JULY 1945

KANZAKI PLANT (Hamilton Type Propellers)
(5) COMMENCED PRODUCTION
(6) FINAL EXPANSION
(7) CAPACITY DECREASE BY DISPERSION AND AIR
    ATTACK OF 15 JUNE 1945

KANZAKI PLANT (V.D.M. Type Propellers)
(8) COMMENCED PRODUCTION
(9) COMMENCED MASS-PRODUCTION
(10) CAPACITY DECREASE BY DISPERSION AND AIR
    ATTACK OF 15 JUNE 1945

SHIZUOKA PLANT (Hamilton Type Propellers)
(11) COMMENCED PRODUCTION
(12) DECREASE IN CAPACITY BECAUSE OF LACK OF
    MACHINE TOOLS
(13) CAPACITY DECREASE BY DISPERSION AND AIR
    ATTACKS OF 24 APRIL AND 20 JUNE 1945

TSU PLANT (Hamilton Type Propellers)
(14) COMMENCED PRODUCTION
(15) DECREASE IN CAPACITY BECAUSE OF LACK OF
    MACHINE TOOLS
(16) CAPACITY DECREASE BY DISPERSION AND AIR
    ATTACK OF 26 JUNE 1945

SUMITOMO, APPENDIX F

SUMITOMO METAL INDUSTRIES

KANZAKI PLANT
(KANZAKI SEISAKUSHO)

PLANT REPORT No. VI—1

TABLE OF CONTENTS

THE PLANT AND ITS FUNCTION IN THE AIRCRAFT INDUSTRY

Introduction

The Kanzaki factory, largest of the four plants of the propeller division of Sumitomo Metal Industries and the largest propeller manufacturer in Japan, was located in Amagasaki (34-44N, 135-25-30E). The main offices and design section of the division were maintained in this plant.

Kanzaki was built in the 3 years preceding the war, commencing operation in April 1941, and contained 129 buildings with a total floor area of 2,414,676 square feet (Appendix A). No major expansion of factory buildings was undertaken after the initial construction of the plant, the increase in production from 1941 to the onset of air raids in 1945 being attributed to increasing skill of the workers and the development of labor-saving jigs and tools. The research section, however, was expanded greatly in 1944 with the completion of the wind tunnel in March and the addition of two new test cells in May. This rendered the research and design section independent of the Sumitomo plant at Sakurajima, whose facilities Kanzaki had been compelled to use up to this time.

There was no connection between the plant and the government except in matters relating to production requirements, and there were no government supervisors at the plant other than the usual Navy and Army inspectors charged with the acceptance or rejection of finished propellers for their respective services. All financial requirements were met by Sumitomo Metal Industries, which in turn was dependent on the Sumitomo Bank. Sumitomo Metal Industries had set aside a fund to be used in the development of propeller designs and major loans for prototype construction of new propellers at Kanzaki were charged against this fund.

Kanzaki produced both the Hamilton standard counterweight type propeller and the Vereinigte Deutsche Metallwerke (VDM) propeller, for which Sumitomo purchased the patents from the United States and Germany respectively. In 1943, about 400 propellers of a modified Hamilton type were produced, 120 of these in June. This propeller had wooden blades and was not acceptable under combat conditions, but was installed in first-line aircraft used as advanced trainers. Production statistics for this propeller are included in the Hamilton type figures. Kanzaki produced propellers for 25 different aircraft (Appendix B).

Plant Organization and Operation

The chief of the Sumitomo Propeller Division, Osamu Sugimoto, was also the head of the Kanzaki plant, and in particular was in charge of the design department there. He had studied aeronautical engineering at the Massachusetts Institute of Technology. Isamu Shirai was chief assistant to Sugimoto both in the Division administration and at Kanzaki. He was especially concerned with business affairs and labor administration and was, in addition, charged with the air-raid defense system of all four plants. Bunzo Hito, a staff member of the Propeller Division, acted as production superintendent at Kanzaki, in general charge of the production, engineering, technical, and inspection departments.

Kanzaki was organized in seven departments: the business department, under Keiichi Wada directly, and ultimately on the divisional and policy making level under Shirai; the labor administration department, under Shirai; the defense department, under Shirai; the production department, under Soji Hori directly and Hito finally; the engineering department, under Hito; the technical department, directed by Sugimoto but administered by Hito; and the inspection department under Hito generally and Inao Yoshida directly (Appendix C).

Production-line technique was used successfully at Kanzaki except that output in relation to available floor area was still low when judged by American standards (Appendix D). Conveyor systems were not used. Many Sumitomo officials had studied mass production methods in America and attempt was made to confine workers to particular jobs and then to develop individual skill ("standardization"). It was felt that sound planning had a beneficial effect on production and on several occasions monthly production increased in spite of an accompanying drop in the number of employees.

Student labor was employed at Kanzaki in April 1944, but, with the exception of discharged men included in workers of civilian status, no soldier labor was used (Figure 1 and Appendix E).

16

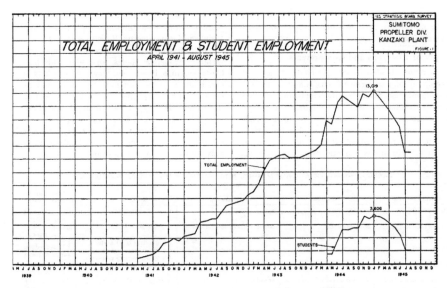

TOTAL EMPLOYMENT & STUDENT EMPLOYMENT
APRIL 1941 - AUGUST 1945

13,019

TOTAL EMPLOYMENT

3,806

STUDENTS

1939 1940 1941 1942 1943 1944 1945

m 1942 until the end of the war Kanzaki ted on two 12-hour shifts, from 0730 to 1930 rom 1930 to 0730. Allowing for meals, the average work-day was 10.2 hours, therefore this figure was used in computing man-hours (Figure 2, Appendix F). Only 15 percent of employees were

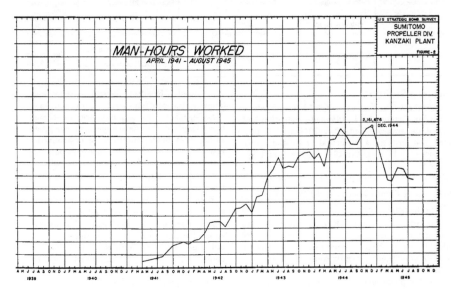

MAN-HOURS WORKED
APRIL 1941 - AUGUST 1945

2,161,676
DEC. 1944

1939 1940 1941 1942 1943 1944 1945

on the night shift and accordingly the main part of the plant—the final assembly shops—was shut down during this period.

Supply of Materials and Components

Raw materials allocations were made at meetings of company and government officials at which the government also presented its short-range (quarterly) requirements and the company requested such assistance as was necessary. When materials were not delivered on time, formal objections were made to the Kinki district office which in turn informed the Munitions Ministry if the matter was not handled satisfactorily. The plant was pendent on over 40 different suppliers for raw : terials and components (Reference Item 1).

The following products were made from raw terials: propeller blades, propeller hub barr blade bushings, liners, counterweight brackets, s] ers, pistons, gears, and miscellaneous small pa Blade, barrel, and propeller assembly for both H ilton and VDM types were done at the plant.

In addition to the use of wooden propeller bla in place of aluminum, shortages of critical mater compelled a number of other substitutions in or that production might continue (Table 1).

TABLE 1.—*Sumitomo Propeller Division, Kanzaki Plant—Use of Substitute Materials*

Original material	Substitute	Where Applied	Reason for use	Development a success of substi
Ni-Cr-Mo Steel..........	Si-Cr-Mu Steel.............	Spider......................	Shortage of Ni & Mo...........	Mass-produced f August 1943.
Ni-Cr-Mo Steel..........	Si-Cr-Mu Steel.............	Barrel, bracket, counterweight, etc.	Shortage of Ni & Mo...........	Mass-produced fi August 1943.
Ni-Cr-Mo Steel..........	Carbon Steel...............	Cylinder head piston, etc.......	1. Shortage of Ni & Mo...... 2. No need for high strength 3. Easier working properties...	Mass-produced from August 1
Case-hardening Steel......	Case hardening Steel........	Gears (VDM)............	Shortage of Ni............	Mass produced f: August 1943.
Light alloy propeller blade..	Wooden propeller blade...... (Schwarz type)	Propeller blade for Ki 51.......	Shortages of Al.............	Mass-produced fr January 1945.
	Wooden propeller blade...... (Hardened wood type).	Propeller blade for Q1W1,...... A6M5, A6M2-K, G4M3.	Shortage of Al..............	Not-mass produc
	Hollow steel propeller blade ..	Propeller blade for H11 K1.....	1. Shortage of Al.......... 2. Superiority in large blades.	Not mass-produ
Be-bronze casting.........	Al-bronze casting..........	Blade bushing...............	Shortage of Be..............	Mass produced 1939.
Al-bronze casting.........	Malleable cast-iron lining of... Al-bronze casting	Blade bushing.............	Shortage of Cu.............	Mass-produced f August 1944.
Leather packing..........	Rubber packing.............	Oil supply line packing........	Shortage of leather..........	Mass-produced f October 1944.
Copper-asbestos packing....	Rubber packing............	Cylinder head packing.........	1. Superiority in preventing oil leakage............. 2. Shortage of Cu and asbestos	Mass-produce from April

Production Statistics

Kanzaki reached peak capacity of 2270 propellers a month in October 1944. Planned production had reached its peak in September 1944 with a projected 3040 propellers but actual production never rose above the 1878 of July 1944 (Figure 3 and Appendix G).

Repair work was not performed at Kanzaki.

Diversion of Plant Capacity and Effort to
Experimental Work

As mentioned above, the Kanzaki plant was the home of the research section of the Sumitomo Propeller Division. Experiments carried out and a complete tabulation of results were as follows:

Aerodynamics. Experiment: To obtain airfoil sections for propellers that would perform best at

high speeds. Results: Several sections were tained which were improvements over current ty

Experiment: To obtain figures on change blade length and to determine optimum pitch. sults: Best blade lengths were determined, retical figures on airfoil ratings were obtained a study was made of heavy-loaded propellers.

Vibration. Experiment: To study the chara istics of propeller blade frequencies. Results:

Experiment: Measurement of the vibi stress of rotating propeller blades. Results:

Propeller Parts. Experiment: To deteri stress distribution along shank and boss of H ton type propeller. Results: Stress diagram obtained by photoelectric and direct measurem

Experiment: To determine the torsional rig of various propeller blades. Results: Figures

18

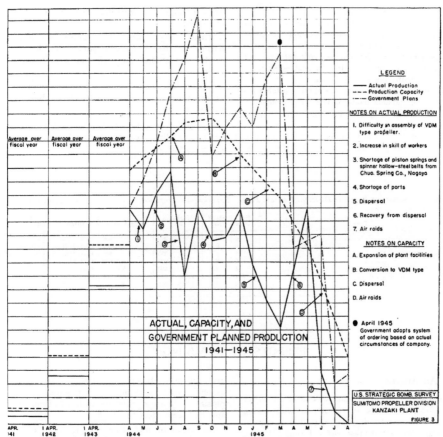

ACTUAL, CAPACITY, AND GOVERNMENT PLANNED PRODUCTION 1941–1945

Average over fiscal year   Average over fiscal year   Average over fiscal year

APR. '41 | APR. 1942 | APR. 1943 | A M J J A S O N D 1944 | J F M A M J J A 1945

ined for several light alloy blades.

xperiment: To determine a suitable lubricant the pitch-control mechanism of the VDM pro-r. Results: A suitable lubricant was discov-

xperiment: To determine the strength of the s of the VDM type propeller boss. Results: was obtained for worm, worm wheel, etc., by eeting parts to centrifugal force and twisting ments.

overning Systems. Experiment: To check the ormance of the Hamilton type governor. Re-: Several dimensions were changed and an im-'ed performance obtained.

Experiment: To improve the electric motors used to change pitch on the VDM type. Results: Useful data obtained.

Experiment: To improve the performance of the oil motors used to change pitch on the VDM type. Results: Useful data obtained.

Experiment. To improve performance of VDM governor. Results: Useful data obtained.

Experiment: To devise a satisfactory feathering mechanism for the VDM propeller. Results: Useful data obtained.

Wooden Propellers. Experiment: To determine strength and fatigue of ordinary and improved plywood blades. Results: Engineering data on neces-

19

sary strengths were obtained.

Experiment: To develop a cement for use around blade shank. Results: A cement suitable for mass production was obtained.

Experiment: To develop a coating to protect blades from weather. Results: A coating suitable for mass production was obtained.

Chemicals. Experiment: To obtain suitable lubricants for various parts of the VDM propeller. Results: Study completed and operating requirements satisfied.

Experiment: To test the possibility of using synthetic rubber as packing. Results: Methods of us-

ing both leather and synthetic rubber packing v developed.

Metals. Experiment: To improve on exis plating. Results: The use of cadmium and its stitutes was studied and reference data was tained.

Experiment: To determine the possibility of ing new types of steel in propeller blades. Rest Data obtained.

In addition to these experiments, seven ex mental propellers were constructed for proto planes (Table 2).

TABLE 2.—*Sumitomo Propeller Division, Kanzaki Plant—Experimental Propellers Constructed for Prototype Pla*

Type	No. Blades	Shank Size	Maximum hp.	Weight (lbs.)	Diameter	N proc
VDM	4	F	3,000	600	14 ft.	
VDM	6	E	3,000	680	12 ft.–13 ft.	
Hamilton (counter-rotating)	4	E	2,800	500	11 ft.–6 in.	
VDM	6	E	3,000	600	11 ft. 6 in.	
VDM and Hamilton (hollow steel)	4	E	2,500	500–600	13 ft.	
VDM and Hamilton (plyWood)	3–4	E	1,000–2,000	300–500	9 ft.–13 ft.	
VDM	3–4	E	1,500–2,000	300–500	10 ft.–13 ft.	

EFFECTS OF BOMBING

The Air Attacks

Although the Kanzaki plant was never the object of a direct air attack, it was struck twice during urban area attacks directed against the city of Nagoya. The first of these was in 1 June 1945. In that 30-minute daylight attack only a few bombs fell into the plant area; none struck buildings or machinery, and no casualties were caused. A loss of 60,330 man-hours resulted, however.

The second attack, on 15 June, was heavy. Approximately 70 percent of the plant buildings were destroyed. Although most of the buildings were of steel frame and corrugated sheet metal construction, fires spread readily since floors were wood-block type and the buildings contained large quantities of inflammable materials such as wooden crates and combustible liquids (Photos 1 to 7). Approximately 39,000 man-hours of labor were required to repair damage to buildings so that some

degree of production could be resumed, and a ditional 78,000 man-hours were required fo repair of damaged machine tools (Append and Reference Item No. 2).

Because of an efficient air-raid precaution s which provided shelter within the plant for al sonnel, casualties were light; three killed an wounded. However, 54,297 man-hours wer because of workers taking shelter.

Production was completely halted by this and dropped to about 24 percent of normal after. The plant was not repaired to any ap able extent thereafter and the war ended l recovery could be made. After this attack officials had hoped to obtain about 65 perc former capacity largely through dispersal.

Man-Hour Losses Caused by Alerts

Air attack alerts in the Nagoya area were n ous. Although the Kanzaki plant was struck

20

Photo 1—Building S-1 (Hub Assembly Shop), looking west.

Photo 2—Building S-2 (Hub Assembly Shop), view of roof.

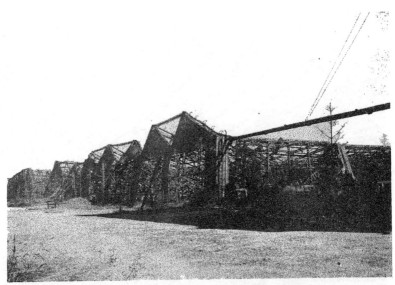

Photo 3—Building S-2 (Hub Assembly Shop), west wall.

Photo 4—Building S-3 (Heat Treatment Shop).

22

Photo 5—Building S-4 (Final Assembly Shop).

Photo 6—Building S-4 (Final Assembly Shop), east wall.

23

Photo 7—Building T (Machine Shop), southwest corner.

twice, the numerous alerts caused extensive losses in man-hours of work. This is shown in Table 3.

TABLE 3.—*Sumitomo Propeller Division, Kanzaki Plant—Man-Hours Lost Due to Air-Raid Alerts*

Month, 1945	Man-hours lost	Percentage of production lost
January	97,893	5
February	58,589	3
March	87,913	7
April	31,512	2.5
May	29,677	1.5
June	42,520	3
July	114,982	9
Total	463,086	4.4

Interruption to Production Due to Area Attacks

Kanzaki never experienced any shortage of electric power. The area raids, however, did have a serious effect upon labor. Apart from casualties, there was a great deal of absenteeism ascribed to workers moving their families to safer areas, workers remaining at home in order to cultivate foodstuffs to offset the destruction of stocks in the raids, crowding of transportation facilities, the loss of many public and private vehicles, an increase in sickness due to exposure and lack of living necessities, and a decline in morale especially among workers who had suffered personal loss.

Interruption of Production Due to Attacks Affecting Suppliers

Starting in March 1945, percentages of receipts against orders dropped steadily until the end of the war both for parts and for raw materials. (Reference Item I, USSBS Aircraft Division Corporation Report No. VI.) Attempts to counteract this were not successful due to the fact that most companies were dispersing simultaneously and could not meet requirements. Whenever possible, government aid was requested and received, but the government program was not coordinated and official emphasis on a particular item usually led only to abnormal drops in the supply of other items.

Dispersal of Plant Operations

In December 1944 the government ordered Sumitomo to disperse its propeller production facilities. Sites were selected during January and February and dispersal took place in March, April, and May 1945 (Table 4 and Appendix H). The six sites selected were well camouflaged, and officials of

24

	Machine tools	No. workers	Distance from Kanzaki	Date started	Percentage completed
			miles		
....	85	500	50	Feb. 45	100
....	50	200	31	Mar. 45	100
....	10	1,000	9	Feb. 45	100
....	0	21	9	Feb. 45	100
....	515	4,000	25	....	30
olling parts					
....	15	210	20	Mar. 45	100

also was shown to suffer from this type of bombing. The immediate cause of deficiency in consignments from suppliers, however, was the inadequate handling of this problem by the government during the dispersal period. The suspension of production during air-raid alerts affected output seriously

The plant was vulnerable potentially to HE bomb attack as well, but its greatest weakness as shown by the record was probably the degree to which shortage of essential parts could reduce production.

GENERAL IMPRESSIONS

Kanzaki was the most important propeller plant in Japan, and occupied a central position due to the presence of division headquarters and research facilities. As a result of incendiary raids it was effectively reduced to a low production figure with no prospect of rapid recovery.

REFERENCE ITEMS

The following material is in the files of USSBS, Aircraft Division, in the Office of the Adjutant General, War Department, Washington, D. C.

REFERENCE ITEM 1: Chart, "Raw Materials and Component Sources," Sumitomo—Kanzaki VI-1.

REFERENCE ITEM 2: Chart, "Machine Tool Sebedule," Sumitomo—Kanzaki VI-1.

25

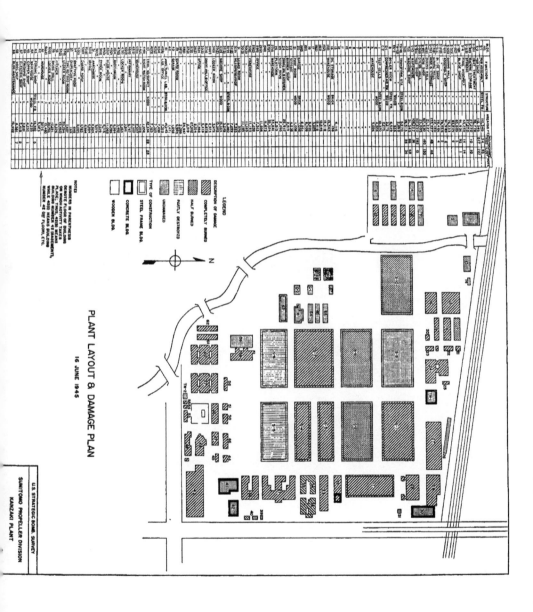

PLANT LAYOUT & DAMAGE PLAN

16 JUNE 1945

U.S. STRATEGIC BOMB. SURVEY
SUMITOMO PROPELLER DIVISION
KANZAKI PLANT

LIST OF PRODUCTS, KANZAKI PLANT, SUMITOMO PROPELLER DIVISION

Type	Aircraft		Company	Shipped to	Branch of Service
H	E13A1	(Jake 11)	Aichi	Nagoya	Navy
H	L2D3	(Tabby 22)	Showa	Showa	Navy
H	P1Y1	(Frances 11)	Nakajima	Koizumi	Navy
H	P1Y1-S	(Frances 11)	Kawanishi	Konan	Navy
H	P1Y1	(Frances)	Kawanishi	Konan	Navy
H	D4Y1	(Judy 11)	Aichi	Nagoya	Navy
H	D4Y2	(Judy 12)	Aichi	Nagoya	Navy
H	D4A1	(exp. July)	Aichi	Nagoya	Navy
H	M6A1	(Seiran)	Aichi	Nagoya	Navy
H	C6N1	(Murt 11)	Nakajima	Koizumi	Navy
H	C6N1	(Myrt 11)	Nakajima	Handa	Navy
H	B6N2	(Jill 12)	Nakajima	Handa	Navy
H	H8K2	(Emily 12)	Kawanishi	Konan	Navy
H	G4M2	(Betty 22)	Mitsubishi	Nagoya	Navy
H	G4M2-A	(Betty 24)	Mitsubishi	Nagoya	Navy
H	G4M2-A	(Betty 24)	Mitsubishi	Mizushima	Navy
H	G4M3	(Betty 34)	Mitsubishi	Nagoya	Navy
H	G4M3	(Betty 34)	Mitsubishi	Mizushima	Navy
H	J2M3	(Jack 21)	Mitsubishi	Nagoya	Navy
H	J2M3	(Jack 21)	Mitsubishi	Suzuka	Navy
H	J2M3	(Jack 21)	Navy	Kosa	Navy
VDM	N1K1-J	(George)	Kawanishi	Naruo	Navy
VDM	N1K1-J	(George)	Kawanishi	Himeji	Navy
VDM	B7A1	(Grace 11)	Aichi	Nagoya	Navy
VDM	J5N1	(Tenrai)	Nakajima	Koizumi	Navy
H	E16A1	(Paul 11)	Aichi	Nagoya	Navy
H	E16A1	(Paul 11)	Nippon Hikoki	Tomioka	Navy
H	D3A2	(Val 22)	Aichi	Nagoya	Navy
VDM	A7M1	(Sam 11)	Mitsubishi	Nagoya	Navy
H	D4Y3	(Judy 33)	Aichi	Nagoya	Navy
VDM	J2M4	(Jack)	Mitsubishi	Suzuka	Navy
VDM	J2M4	(Jack)	Mitsubishi	Kosa	Navy
VDM	N1K2-J	(George 21)	Mitsubishi	Mizushima	Navy
VDM	N1K2-J	(George 21)	Aichi	Nagoya	Navy
VDM	N1K2-J	(George 21)	Kawanishi	Naruo	Navy
VDM	N1K2-J	(George 21)	Kawanishi	Himeji	Navy
VDM	N1K2-J	(George 21)	Showa	Showa	Navy
VDM	N1K2-J	(George 21)	Navy	Kosa	Navy
H	D3Y1	(exp. Val)	Experimental		
VDM	J2M5	(Jack)	Mitsubishi	Nagoya	Navy
VDM	J2M5	(Jack)	Mitsubishi	Suzuka	Navy
VDM	Ki-67	(Peggy)		Kagamigahara	Army
VDM	Ki-74	(Patsy)		Tachikawa	Army
VDM	Ki-83			Kagamigahara	Army

s.—All Army propellers were shipped to Army Air Arsenals, not to manufacturers.

ous blade–and–shank size combinations were used on different aircraft. See Appendix A basic Report VI.
Hamilton-type propeller; VDM—Vereingte Deutsche Mettallwerks type propeller.

APPENDIX C

KANZAKI PLANT, SUMITOMO PROPELLER DIVISION

DEPARTMENTAL ORGANIZATION

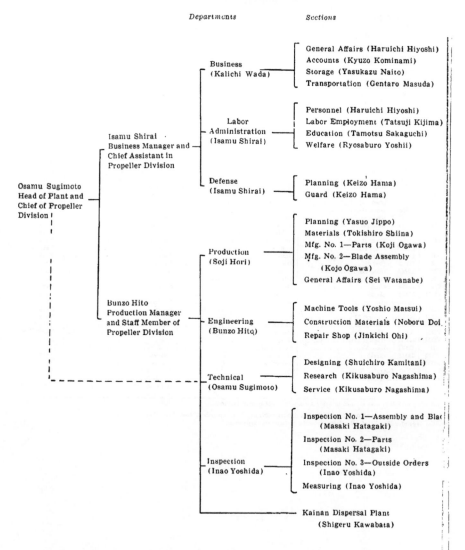

Departments   *Sections*

Business (Kalichi Wada)
- General Affairs (Haruichi Hiyoshi)
- Accounts (Kyuzo Kominami)
- Storage (Yasukazu Naito)
- Transportation (Gentaro Masuda)

Labor Administration (Isamu Shirai)
- Personnel (Haruichi Hiyoshi)
- Labor Employment (Tatsuji Kijima)
- Education (Tamotsu Sakaguchi)
- Welfare (Ryosaburo Yoshii)

Defense (Isamu Shirai)
- Planning (Keizo Hama)
- Guard (Keizo Hama)

Isamu Shirai Business Manager and Chief Assistant in Propeller Division

Osamu Sugimoto Head of Plant and Chief of Propeller Division

Production (Soji Hori)
- Planning (Yasuo Jippo)
- Materials (Tokishiro Shiina)
- Mfg. No. 1—Parts (Koji Ogawa)
- Mfg. No. 2—Blade Assembly (Kojo Ogawa)
- General Affairs (Sei Watanabe)

Engineering (Bunzo Hito)
- Machine Tools (Yoshio Matsui)
- Construction Materials (Noboru Doi)
- Repair Shop (Jinkichi Ohi)

Bunzo Hito Production Manager and Staff Member of Propeller Division

Technical (Osamu Sugimoto)
- Designing (Shuichiro Kamitani)
- Research (Kikusaburo Nagashima)
- Service (Kikusaburo Nagashima)

Inspection (Inao Yoshida)
- Inspection No. 1—Assembly and Blac (Masaki Hatagaki)
- Inspection No. 2—Parts (Masaki Hatagaki)
- Inspection No. 3—Outside Orders (Inao Yoshida)
- Measuring (Inao Yoshida)

Kainan Dispersal Plant (Shigeru Kawabata)

28

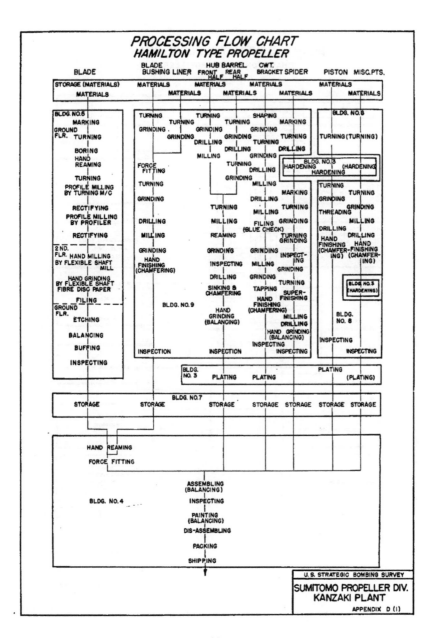

PROCESSING FLOW CHART
HAMILTON TYPE PROPELLER

U. S. STRATEGIC BOMBING SURVEY

SUMITOMO PROPELLER DIV.
KANZAKI PLANT

APPENDIX D (I)

29

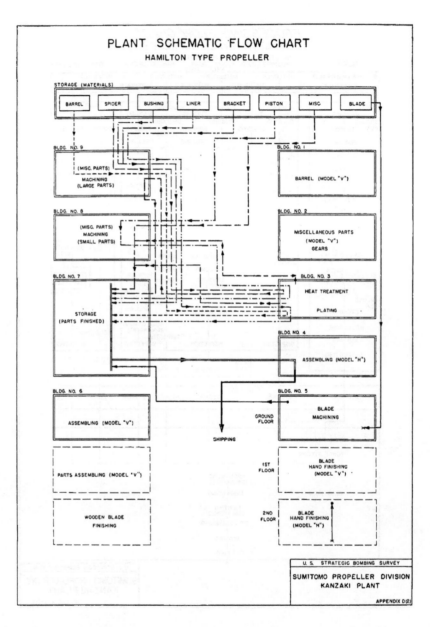

PLANT SCHEMATIC FLOW CHART
HAMILTON TYPE PROPELLER

STORAGE (MATERIALS)

| BARREL | SPIDER | BUSHING | LINER | BRACKET | PISTON | MISC | BLADE |

BLDG. NO. 9
(MISC. PARTS)
MACHINING
(LARGE PARTS)

BLDG. NO. 1
BARREL (MODEL "V")

BLDG. NO. 8
(MISC. PARTS)
MACHINING
(SMALL PARTS)

BLDG. NO. 2
MISCELLANEOUS PARTS
(MODEL "V")
GEARS

BLDG. NO. 7
STORAGE
(PARTS FINISHED)

BLDG. NO. 3
HEAT TREATMENT
PLATING

BLDG. NO. 4
ASSEMBLING (MODEL "H")

BLDG. NO. 6
ASSEMBLING (MODEL "V")

GROUND FLOOR

SHIPPING

BLDG. NO. 5
BLADE
MACHINING

PARTS ASSEMBLING (MODEL "V")

1ST FLOOR
BLADE
HAND FINISHING
(MODEL "V")

WOODEN BLADE
FINISHING

2ND FLOOR
BLADE
HAND FINISHING
(MODEL "H")

U. S. STRATEGIC BOMBING SURVEY
SUMITOMO PROPELLER DIVISION
KANZAKI PLANT
APPENDIX D(2)

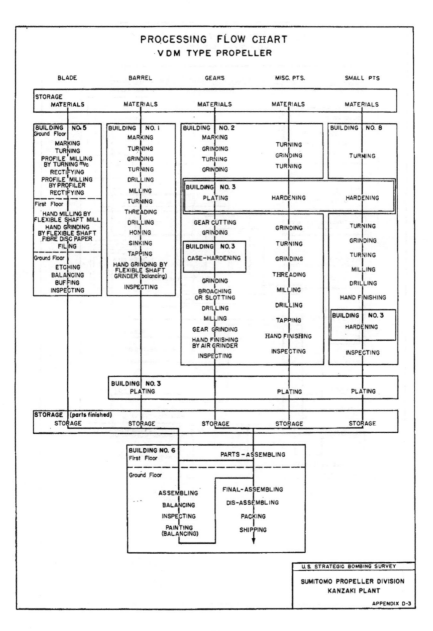

PROCESSING FLOW CHART
VDM TYPE PROPELLER

| BLADE | BARREL | GEARS | MISC. PTS. | SMALL PTS |

STORAGE

| MATERIALS | MATERIALS | MATERIALS | MATERIALS | MATERIALS |

BUILDING NO. 5 — Ground Floor
- MARKING
- TURNING
- PROFILE MILLING BY TURNING mvc
- RECTIFYING
- PROFILE MILLING BY PROFILER
- RECTIFYING

First Floor
- HAND MILLING BY FLEXIBLE SHAFT MILL
- HAND GRINDING BY FLEXIBLE SHAFT
- FIBRE DISC PAPER
- FILING

Ground Floor
- ETCHING
- BALANCING
- BUFFING
- INSPECTING

BUILDING NO. I
- MARKING
- TURNING
- GRINDING
- TURNING
- DRILLING
- MILLING
- TURNING
- THREADING
- DRILLING
- HONING
- SINKING
- TAPPING
- HAND GRINDING BY FLEXIBLE SHAFT GRINDER (balancing)
- INSPECTING

BUILDING NO. 2
- MARKING
- GRINDING
- TURNING
- GRINDING

BUILDING NO. 3
- PLATING

- GEAR CUTTING
- GRINDING

BUILDING NO. 3
- CASE–HARDENING

- GRINDING
- BROACHING OR SLOTTING
- DRILLING
- MILLING
- GEAR GRINDING
- HAND FINISHING BY AIR GRINDER
- INSPECTING

- TURNING
- GRINDING
- TURNING

HARDENING

- GRINDING
- TURNING
- GRINDING
- THREADING
- MILLING
- DRILLING
- TAPPING
- HAND FINISHING
- INSPECTING

BUILDING NO. 8
- TURNING

HARDENING

- TURNING
- GRINDING
- TURNING
- MILLING
- DRILLING
- HAND FINISHING

BUILDING NO. 3
- HARDENING

- INSPECTING

BUILDING NO. 3
- PLATING

| | PLATING | PLATING |

STORAGE (parts finished)

| STORAGE | STORAGE | STORAGE | STORAGE | STORAGE |

BUILDING NO. 6 — First Floor

PARTS – ASSEMBLING

Ground Floor
- ASSEMBLING
- BALANCING
- INSPECTING
- PAINTING (BALANCING)

- FINAL-ASSEMBLING
- DIS-ASSEMBLING
- PACKING
- SHIPPING

31

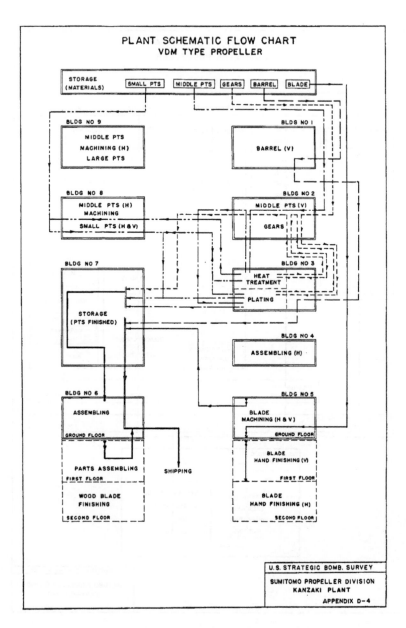

PLANT SCHEMATIC FLOW CHART
VDM TYPE PROPELLER

STORAGE (MATERIALS) · SMALL PTS · MIDDLE PTS · GEARS · BARREL · BLADE

BLDG NO 9
MIDDLE PTS
MACHINING (H)
LARGE PTS

BLDG NO 1
BARREL (V)

BLDG NO 8
MIDDLE PTS (H)
MACHINING
SMALL PTS (H & V)

BLDG NO 2
MIDDLE PTS (V)
GEARS

BLDG NO 7

BLDG NO 3
HEAT TREATMENT
PLATING

STORAGE (PTS FINISHED)

BLDG NO 4
ASSEMBLING (H)

BLDG NO 6
ASSEMBLING
GROUND FLOOR

PARTS ASSEMBLING
FIRST FLOOR

WOOD BLADE FINISHING
SECOND FLOOR

SHIPPING

BLDG NO 5
BLADE MACHINING (H & V)
GROUND FLOOR

BLADE HAND FINISHING (V)
FIRST FLOOR

BLADE HAND FINISHING (H)
SECOND FLOOR

U.S. STRATEGIC BOMB. SURVEY

SUMITOMO PROPELLER DIVISION
KANZAKI PLANT

APPENDIX D-4

APPENDIX E

Employment Statistics, April 1941–August 1945—Kanzaki Plant, Sumitomo Propeller Division

Month	Regular workers			Students			Total			Direct-Indirect			Newly hired		
	Men	Women	Total	Men	Women	Total	Men	Women	Total	Prod.	Non-P.	Total	Men	Women	Total
1941															
il..........	422	27	449				422	27	449	375	74	449	10	5	15
/...........	532	35	567				532	35	567	475	92	567	8	3	11
B...........	620	43	663				620	43	663	554	109	663	44	8	52
'...........	758	54	812				758	54	812	694	118	812	43	8	51
ust.........	1,025	108	1,133				1,025	108	1,133	962	171	1,133	108	43	151
tember......	1,503	177	1,680				1,503	177	1,680	1,453	227	1,680	287	66	353
ober........	1,662	184	1,846				1,662	184	1,846	1,620	226	1,846	163	33	196
ember......	1,845	199	2,044				1,845	199	2,044	1,810	234	2,044	115	25	140
ember.......	1,743	180	1,923				1,743	180	1,923	1,706	217	1,923	28	9	37
1942															
un.y........	1,915	198	2,113				1,915	198	2,113	1,877	236	2,113	53	18	71
ruary.......	1,992	212	2,204				1,992	212	2,204	1,958	246	2,204	44	19	63
ch..........	2,035	259	2,294				2,035	259	2,294	2,002	292	2,294	54	21	75
il..........	2,854	309	3,163				2,854	309	3,163	2,804	359	3,163	419	83	502
/...........	2,977	325	3,302				2,977	325	3,302	2,914	388	3,302	365	28	393
B...........	3,126	326	3,452				3,126	326	3,452	3,052	400	3,452	160	21	181
'...........	3,170	338	3,508				3,170	338	3,508	3,088	420	3,508	74	16	90
ust.........	3,642	376	4,018				3,642	376	4,018	3,529	489	4,018	381	20	401
tember......	4,241	385	4,626				4,241	385	4,626	4,097	529	4,626	644	15	659
ober........	4,320	398	4,718				4,320	398	4,718	4,161	557	4,718	57	3	60
ember......	4,382	403	4,785				4,382	403	4,785	4,220	565	4,785	56	10	66
ember.......	4,463	407	4,870				4,463	407	4,870	4,295	575	4,870	61	9	70
1943															
uary........	4,736	424	5,160				4,736	424	5,160	4,552	608	5,160	61	14	75
ruary.......	5,185	437	5,622				5,185	437	5,622	4,977	645	5,622	79	35	114
ch..........	5,660	486	6,146				5,660	486	6,146	5,441	705	6,146	652	54	706
il..........	6,570	558	7,128				6,570	558	7,128	6,315	813	7,128	483	74	557
/...........	7,318	582	7,900				7,318	582	7,900	7,031	869	7,900	178	36	214
B...........	7,434	582	8,016				7,434	582	8,016	7,142	784	8,016	112	16	128
'...........	7,627	594	8,221				7,627	594	8,221	7,339	882	8,221	88	14	102
ust.........	7,655	598	8,253				7,655	598	8,253	7,359	894	8,253	202	8	210
tember......	7,528	594	8,122				7,528	594	8,122	7,245	877	8,122	43	7	50
ober........	7,499	588	8,087				7,499	588	8,087	7,223	864	8,087	66	11	77
ember......	7,463	602	8,065				7,463	602	8,065	7,195	870	8,065	87	16	103
ember.......	7,697	590	8,287				7,697	590	8,287	7,401	886	8,287	286	20	306
1944															
uary........	7,846	599	8,445				7,846	599	8,445	7,547	898	8,445	238	11	249
ruary.......	7,939	678	8,617				7,939	678	8,617	7,700	917	8,617	81	19	100
ch..........	8,706	941	9,147				8,206	941	9,147	8,027	1,120	9,147	152	104	256
il..........	8,766	1,400	10,166	285	383	668	9,051	1,783	10,834	9,574	1,260	10,834	1,166	1,048	2,214
/...........	8,583	1,427	10,010	315	383	698	8,898	1,810	10,708	9,383	1,325	10,708	76	73	149
B...........	8,877	1,472	10,349	756	993	1,749	9,633	2,465	12,098	10,666	1,432	12,098	706	442	1,148
'...........	8,590	1,489	10,079	1,507	990	2,497	10,097	2,479	12,576	11,146	1,430	12,576	1,062	256	1,318
ust.........	8,346	1,484	9,830	1,554	976	2,530	9,900	2,460	12,360	10,939	1,421	12,360	148	28	174
tember......	8,083	1,463	9,546	1,583	1,094	2,677	9,666	2,557	12,223	10,821	1,402	12,223	159	155	314
ober........	7,718	1,490	9,208	1,601	1,085	2,686	9,319	2,575	11,894	10,468	1,429	11,894	124	23	147
ember......	7,594	1,710	9,304	1,792	1,770	3,562	9,386	3,480	12,866	11,398	1,468	12,866	262	775	1,037
ember.......	7,476	1,735	9,211	1,775	1,763	3,538	9,251	3,498	12,749	11,285	1,462	12,747	30	248	278
1945															
uary........	7,588	1,825	9,413	1,734	1,872	3,606	9,322	3,397	13,019	11,428	1,591	13,019	194	225	419
ruary.......	7,385	1,890	9,275	1,710	1,850	3,560	9,095	3,740	12,835	11,270	1,565	12,835	63	43	106
ch..........	6,957	1,779	8,736	1,750	1,712	3,462	8,707	3,491	12,198	10,632	1,566	12,198	5	9	14
il..........	6,767	1,873	8,640	1,809	1,362	3,171	8,576	3,325	11,811	10,233	1,578	11,811	31	89	120
/...........	6,496	1,912	8,408	1,460	1,294	2,754	7,956	3,206	11,162	9,565	1,597	11,162	90	97	187
B...........	6,387	1,920	8,307	819	1,294	2,113	7,206	3,214	10,420	8,830	1,590	10,420	5	31	36
'...........	5,865	1,925	7,790	135	823	958	6,000	2,748	8,748	7,163	1,585	8,748	1	2	3
ust.........	5,865	1,925	7,790	135	823	958	6,000	2,748	8,748	7,163	1,585	8,748	......	......	......

early turnover: 1941, 81 percent; 1942, 73 percent; 1943, 35 percent; 1944, 65 percent; 1945, 6 percent.

33

APPENDIX F

Man-Hours Worked, April 1941–August 1945, Kanzaki Plant, Sumitomo Propeller Division

Month	Men	Women	Total	Month	Men	Women	Total
1941				June	1,590,809	69,706	1,660,51
April	84,854	3,357	88,211	July	1,454,913	65,025	1,519,93
May	102,063	4,112	106,175	August	1,493,367	64,890	1,558,25
June	131,041	5,283	136,324	September	1,484,333	62,691	1,547,02
July	141,461	4,963	146,424	October	1,591,805	65,747	1,657,55
August	164,144	6,848	170,992	November	1,676,733	66,404	1,743,13
September	246,799	14,139	260,938	December	1,703,635	71,547	1,775,18
October	305,429	20,356	325,785	**1944**			
November	366,016	22,805	388,821	January	1,593,681	64,785	1,658,46
December	374,187	24,450	398,637	February	1,680,872	69,319	1,750,19
1942				March	1,451,840	75,721	1,537,56
January	369,062	22,909	391,971	April	1,752,665	167,836	1,920,50
February	409,756	24,087	433,843	May	1,726,713	223,165	1,949,87
March	416,956	28,786	445,742	June	1,872,806	244,985	2,117,79
April	478,807	36,042	514,849	July	1,765,593	242,326	2,007,91
May	612,944	43,995	656,939	August	1,627,132	253,076	1,880,20
June	633,402	43,775	680,177	September	1,603,708	256,112	1,859,82
July	634,698	46,849	681,547	October	1,699,429	277,558	1,976,98
August	585,116	45,582	630,698	November	1,794,484	303,337	2,097,82
September	730,425	49,151	779,576	December	1,815,856	345,820	2,161,67
October	867,946	51,927	919,873	**1945**			
November	889,482	49,785	939,267	January	1,661,897	338,750	2,000,64
December	938,789	52,464	991,253	February	1,427,659	308,999	1,736,65
1943				March	1,099,309	248,668	1,347,97
January	870,639	44,937	915,576	April	1,059,249	269,525	1,328,77
February	1,019,757	48,375	1,068,132	May	1,163,725	299,231	1,462,95
March	1,043,817	50,056	1,093,873	June	1,146,538	300,480	1,447,01
April	1,302,552	62,256	1,364,808	July	1,054,198	301,262	1,355,46
May	1,448,231	66,167	1,514,398	August	1,054,796	300,058	1,354,85

APPENDIX G

Actual, Planned, and Capacity Production Statistics, April 1941–August 1945—Kanzaki Plant, Sumitomo Prop Division

Period	Hamilton type			VDM type					
	Actual	Government plan	Capacity	A	GP	C	A	GP	
Fiscal year:									
April 1941–March 1942	680	....	1,469	0	....	30	680	....	
April 1942–March 1943	4,200	....	5,039	70	....	1,030	4,260	....	
April 1943–March 1944	11,450	....	13,147	850	....	2,800	12,300	....	1
1944									
April	1,350	1,250	1,532	253	350	350	1,603	1,603	
May	1,199	1,350	1,595	250	450	370	1,449	1,800	
June	1,308	1,490	1,655	404	570	390	1,712	2,060	
July	1,422	1,635	1,720	456	825	510	1,878	2,460	
August	807	1,665	1,800	305	1,030	430	1,112	2,695	
September	1,146	1,810	1,800	458	1,230	450	1,604	3,040	
October	1,139	1,291	1,800	220	687	470	1,359	1,978	
November	981	1,358	1,670	401	830	490	1,382	2,188	
December	1,012	1,362	1,500	576	995	510	1,588	2,357	
1945									
January	806	1,297	1,374	359	915	530	1,165	2,212	
February	677	1,463	1,250	230	1,095	543	907	2,558	
March	632	1,530	1,120	91	1,220	560	723	2,750	
Fiscal year:									
April 1944–March 1945	12,479	17,501	18,816	4,003	10,197	5,503	16,482	27,701	2
1945									
April	644	705	920	490	600	580	1,134	1,305	
May	932	595	730	656	760	600	1,588	1,355	
June	64	500	587	313	910	470	377	1,410	
July	40	300	444	70	0	340	110	300	
August	....	270	300	....	100	200	....	370	
April–August 1945	1,680	2,370	2,981	1,529	2,370	2,190	3,209	4,740	
Grand total	30,489	(19,871)	41,452	6,442	(12,567)	11,553	36,931	(32,441)	

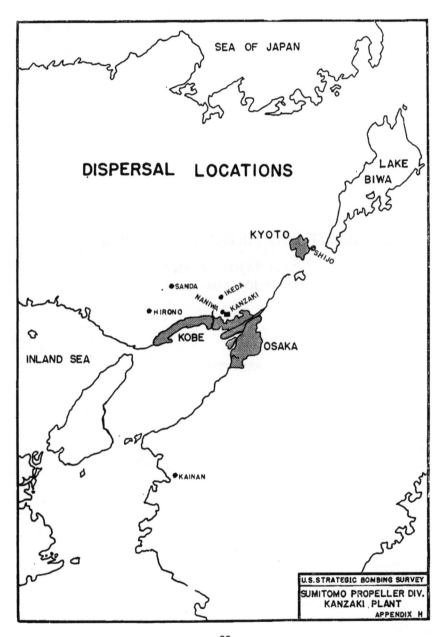

DISPERSAL LOCATIONS

SEA OF JAPAN

LAKE
BIWA

KYOTO
●SHIJO

●SANDA   ●IKEDA
NANIWA   ●KANZAKI
●HIRONO

KOBE

OSAKA

INLAND SEA

●KAINAN

U.S. STRATEGIC BOMBING SURVEY
SUMITOMO PROPELLER DIV.
KANZAKI PLANT
APPENDIX H

SUMITOMO METAL INDUSTRIES

SAKURAJIMA PLANT
(SAKURAJIMA SEISAKUSHO)

PLANT REPORT No. VI—2

TABLE OF CONTENTS

THE PLANT AND ITS FUNCTION IN THE AIRCRAFT INDUSTRY

Introduction

The Sakurajima plant of the Sumitomo Metal Industries was located in the harbor district of Osaka to the southwest of the town area. The plant buildings formed a group comprising the southeastern section of the Sumitomo Copper Plant (Sumitomo Shindosho), and were situated on reclaimed land to the north of the Aji River.

Of the two largest buildings of the 36 constituting the plant, one was utilized as a blade machining and assembly shop, and the other as a boss and hub shop. The remainder, all relatively smaller, were variously utilized as offices, warehouses and machine shops (Appendix A). The total floor area of the Sakurajima plant was 535,024 square feet.

Sumitomo Metal Industries commenced the manufacture of metal alloy propellers in 1933 at the Sakurajima Copper Works. From this date until 1937 the manufacture of propellers was the responsibility of the copper plant. By 1937 so much emphasis had been brought to bear upon the future importance of propeller production that an independent division known as the Propeller Division was formed. This division became one of the six which, together, constituted the Sumitomo Metal Industries (Table 1) and had its main office and plant located in the section of the copper works formerly utilized ·by that division for propeller manufacture.

TABLE 1—*Organization of the Sumitomo Metal Industries Ltd.*

Sumitomo Metal Industries Ltd.
- Iron Plant (Seikosho)
- Steel Pipe Plant (Kokan Seizosho)
- Nagoya Light Metal Plant (Nagoya Keigokin Seizosho)
- Wakayama Iron and Steel Plant (Wakayama Seitetsusho)
- Copper Plant (Shindosho)
- Propeller Division (Puropera Seizubu). Main office and plant at Kanzaki.

Concurrently with the establishment of an independent propeller division, construction of a new propeller plant at Kanzaki, 1 mile north of Amagasaki and about 5 miles northwest of Osaka, was undertaken. From 1937 until the completion of the Kanzaki plant and the transfer of the main office of the Propeller Division from Sakurajima to Kanzaki in 1941, the Sakurajima plant was subordinate to the main plant at Kanzaki, and equal to that of the two newly instituted Sumitomo propeller plants at Tsu and Shizuoka (Table 1).

Had it not been for dispersal and bomb damage, it was intended that the plants at Sakurajima, Tsu, and Shizuoka should ultimately attain a status equal to that of the Kanzaki plant. During June and July 1945 dispersal of the Sakurajima plant was effected to three locations in the Osaka area. Propeller assembly and some machining functions were transferred to a section of a brewery taken over from the Union Beer Co. at Nishinomiya, 8 miles west of Osaka. The main office of the Sakurajima plant was moved in June 1945, together with most of the machine tool equipment, to the basements of two large department stores, Sogo and Matsuzakaya, in Osaka city itself.

The Sakurajima plant was purely a productive unit during the period 1941-45, with all design experimental and research activities concentrated at the Kanzaki plant.

Other than for monthly government production orders and governmental supervision of raw materials and small parts supply and allocation, all financial and administrative supervision was exercised by the Sumitomo Metal Industries Ltd through its Propeller Division.

In the middle of 1945 the Munitions Ministry allotted secret code numbers to all aircraft plants in Japan. The original Sakurajima plant was given the designation, "Shimbu No. 1085," while dispersal plants at the Sogo and Matsuzakaya department stores were allotted the code groups, "Shimbu 1851" and "Shimbu 1852," respectively. Government inspectors and supervisors stationed at the Sakurajima plant were Captain Futoshi Shimokawa (Navy) and Major Juichi Yano (Army). Two other officers completed the staff of ministerial supervisors.

During the period July 1943-July 1945 the Sakurajima works produced Hamilton Staudard type propellers for Zeke, Lorna, Jake, Tabby and Sonia type aircraft. Although mass production of Vereinigte Deutsche Metallwerke (VDM) type propellers never took place at the Sakurajima plant

38

propellers of the VDM type were assembled ere during the period 1940-42.

rganization and Operation

Because the Sakurajima plant was purely a pro- ductive unit, the greater part of the organization was engaged in direct labor with correspondingly small administrative and clerical departments (Table 2 and Figure 1).

TABLE 2—*Organization of the Sakurajima Plant*

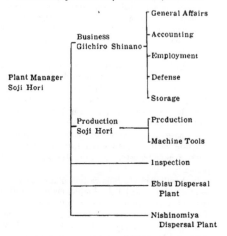

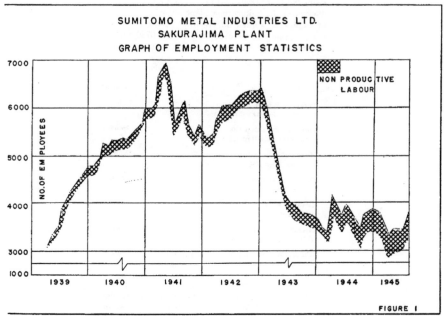

FIGURE I

39

The flow of production from incoming storage was divided into five principal groups: blades, barrels, gears, miscellaneous parts, and small parts. These in turn progressed through various machining processes and after inspection were stored prior to final assembly, balancing, inspection, disassembly and shipping of the completed propeller. The production flow at the Sakurajima plant was generally comparable to those at the other Sumitomo Propeller plants.

It will be noted (Figure 1) that the Sakurajima plant commenced production in 1939 with about 3,000 employees. By May 1941 employment totalled almost 7,000 personnel but declined shortly thereafter due to the transfer of over 1,000 workers to staff the newly constructed Kanzaki plant. The most noticeable decline in manpower, however, occurred early in 1943 when approximately 2,000 workers were transferred to the Tsu and Shizuoka plants.

In April 1944 the Sakurajima plant commenced employing student labor. Employment of students reached a maximum of about 800 early in 1945. The 12-hour shifts were worked daily, from 0730 to 1930 hours, and from 1930 to 0730 hours. It was estimated that throughout the whole period of production at the Sakurajima plant about 85 percent of employees worked on the 0730-1930 shift with the remaining 15 percent on the 1930-0730 shift. No soldiers were employed at the plant at any time.

TABLE 3—*Flow of Small Par*

Name of firm	Location
Terauchi Works (Terauchi Seisakusho KK)	Kyoto
Ishiwaki Precision Co. (Ishiwaki Seimitsu KK)	Osaka
Honda Heavy Industries (Honda Juko KK)	Osaka
Chuo Spring Cox (Chuo Hatsujo KK)	Nagoya
Daido Steel Co. (Daido Seiko KK)	Tokyo
Mitsubishi Steel Co. (Mitsubishi Seiko KK)	Tokyo
About 130 small machine shops in the Osaka area producing rough turnings.	Osaka

With the exception of such items as special screws, piston springs, and sundry small parts, the machining and finishing of all parts delivered in

2). During most of 1944 output exceeded ministerial orders but lagged behind for the first half of 1945 (Fig. 2). The first significant drop in production occurred in February 1945 and was caused by a short supply of small parts. After a recovery in May 1945 further decreases in output were caused by dispersal activities which started in June.

The maximum capacity of the Sakurajima plant was attained in July 1944 and remained at this level until November 1944. Production peaks in January and May 1945 (Fig. 2) were far in excess of capacity because in these months large shipments of small parts were received. Lack of these parts had caused output to fall in December 1944 and during February, March, and April 1945.

Comparison of the production and employment figures for 1941 and 1944 shows that during the latter year twice the output was achieved with half the manpower. This can be explained by the following:

(a) Government orders were small and pressure of work low in 1941.

(b) A larger percentage of skilled workers was being employed in 1944.

(c) Better production methods utilized resulted in increased efficiency.

Rebuilding and Repair of Propellers

No damaged propellers were returned to the Sakurajima plant for repair. Mr. Morita, business affairs manager at the Tsu works, stated that the Army and Navy undertook the repair of damaged propellers at air depots under their own control.

Diversion to Experimental Development

No experimentation or research took place at the Sakurajima plant. Sumitomo's research activities were concentrated at the Kanzaki plant.

ATTACK DATA

INTELLIGENCE DATA:

Date of attack	26 June 1945	24 July 1945
Duration	1026-1202	1251-1322
Attacking Unit	20 AF	20 AF
Altitude	19,000-25,300	19,900-22,100
Number of aircraft over target	64	83
HE dropped	382 tons	494 tons
HE-fusing	Inst. nose, non-delay tail.	Inst. nose, non-delay tail.

EFFECTS OF BOMBING

The Air Attacks

The Sakurajima plant and the Sumitomo copper plant together formed what appeared to be a single group of factory buildings, and photo interpretation never successfully defined the boundaries of each. This target was listed in the Air Objective Folder as 90.25-263A. It was first attacked on 26 June 1945 but all the bombs that did fall within the target area hit the copper plant and left the propeller plant untouched. A second raid on 24 July 1945 almost completely destroyed the Sakurajima plant (Photos 1-2) as well as the copper plant but direct effects upon propeller production were small. All but 27 machine tools (Reference Item 1) had been dispersed by this date and the bombs fell on almost empty buildings.

In only one attack, other than that of 24 July 1945, did bombs fall on the Sakurajima plant. This occurred during an attack on the Osaka urban area on 1 June 1945. A small number of IBs fell within the plant site (Appendix A) and slight damage was caused.

No figures regarding the destruction of raw materials, supplies and finished products were available but a general estimate, made by Sumitomo officials, was that approximately 40 percent of stores and finished products not yet dispersed from the Sakurajima works at the time of the 24 July raid were destroyed. After the 24 July raid no repair of damage was undertaken.

A part of the Sakurajima works was dispersed to a brewery at Nishinomiya in July 1945. As result of the 6 August incendiary raid on the Nishinomiya urban area, sections of the brewery taken over by Sumitomo were destroyed and production brought to a standstill (Appendix B and Reference Item 1).

The following are the casualty figures suffered at the Sakurajima works and the Nishinomiya plant

	Fatalities	Injured	Total
Sakurajima works:			
1 June 1945	2	14	16
24 July 1945	11	10	21
Nishinomiya plant, 6 August 1945	0	0	0

Photo 1—General view of Sakurajima plant, area damaged by the 24 July 1945 attack, looking south towards the hub sho

oto 2—Interior view of the Sakurajima plant hub shop damaged by the 24 July 1945 attack.

▪untermeasures

A unit known as ·the Special Air-Raid Defense rps and consisting of about 20 percent of t1e ▪ailable labor force was formed at eac1 Sumitomo ▪opeller plant for t1e purpose of insuring ade- ▪ate defense measures during alerts and raids. ▪e plant area was subdivided into 10 districts ▪ch under t1e control of an air-raid defense squad. ▪ese squads were in turn responsible to a central ▪adquarters. The 1eadquarters also controlled ▪tions in charge of communications, information, ▪neral affairs and equipment.

The squads in eac1 of t1e 10 plant districts con- ▪ted of fire-fig1ting, relief,. construction, and ▪nsportation units. The relief units were staffed ▪ doctors, nurses, and ot1er medical personnel. ▪e construction units were responsible for effect- ▪g temporary repairs in t1e event t1at specialists ▪m t1e gas, electric power, and water suppliers ▪re not called in. Observation towers and s1elters ▪re distributed t1roug1out t1e plant area.

Interruptions Due to Alerts

Man-1ours lost because of air raid alerts resulted in losses in production as indicated below:

1945	PERCENT
January	2.8
February	2.0
March	4.0
April	1.5
May	1.5
June	1.9
July	7.0
August	2.8

Interruptions Due to Area Attacks

Despite t1ree attacks on t1e Osaka urban area in t1e first 1alf of June 1945, plant officials stated t1at only in isolated cases did t1ese attacks cause any serious interruptions to production. Sources of electric power were not affected and minor dis- ruption in t1e transportation of workers to and from t1e plant lasted only 2 or 3 days.

Interruptions to Supplies

Only in six principal cases (Table 4) was produc-

43

TABLE 4.—*Interruptions to production due to lack of components*

Supplier	Location	Cause of Interruption	Products	Period of Interruption
Terauchi Plant (Terauchi Seisakusho Kk)	Kyoto	Dispersal	Hollow and small screws.	March–April 1945
Honda Heavy Industries Ltd. (Honda Juko Kk)	Osaka	Air attack	Micarta barrel supports.	July–August 1945
Lignite Industries Ltd. (Rigunaito Kogyo Kk)	Osaka	Lack of coal from Yangcheng in North China	Raw micarta	
Chuo Spring Co. (Chuo Hatsujo Kk)	Nagoya	Air attack	Piston springs	February–August
Daido Steel Co. (Daido Seiko Kk)	Tokyo	Urban area attacks caused transportation hold-up from Tokyo	Piston springs	May–August 1945
Mitsubishi Steel Co. (Mitsubishi Seiko Kk)				

tion at the Sakurajima works affected by the lack of components from subcontractors and suppliers.

The Air Ordnance Bureau of the Munitions Ministry gave assistance to Sumitomo only in cases where a bottleneck was caused by lack of large semifinished parts such as blades, spiders, and hubs. In all the shortages listed (Table 4), bottlenecks were caused by small parts such as screws, springs, etc. In such cases the government made no effort to make good the shortages and Sumitomo was left entirely on its own with regard to finding an alternate source.

One such instance was related by Sumitomo officials. The Terauchi plant normally supplied Sumitomo with approximately 70 percent of its hollow screw requirements, the remaining 30 percent being supplied by the Ishiwaki Precision Co. Upon decrease of supply from the Terauchi plant in March 1945, Ishiwaki was unable to increase its output to more than 45 percent of Sumitomo requirements. This caused hollow screws to become a bottleneck until Terauchi managed to regain its former output in June 1945.

Similarly when the supply of piston springs from the Chuo Spring Co. dwindled in March 1945 because of bomb damage, Sumitomo called upon the Daido Steel Co. and the Mitsubishi Steel Co., both in Tokyo, to make good the shortage. Supplies from these two firms in Tokyo were in turn considerably delayed by transportation conditions caused by urban raids along the Tokaido railroad.

Percentages of raw materials and parts ordered which were actually received declined rapidly with the progress of the war. In July 1944, 66 percent of raw materials and 94 percent of parts ordered were delivered by suppliers to Sumitomo, whereas by July 1945, only 16 percent of ordered quantities of raw materials and 36 percent of parts ordered were received (Aircraft Division Corporation Report No. VI, Reference Item 1).

Dispersal

Early in June 1945 the Sakurajima works dispersed to three sites in the Osaka area (Appen C). Two of these were in the basements of two the largest department stores in Osaka (Photo and 4) and the third was located in a section of Union Beer Brewery at Nishinomiya, about 8 m west of Osaka. The sites in the basements of Sogo and Matsuzakaya department stores (Phc 5 to 10) were utilized as machine shops, the fori for large parts such as bosses, spiders, and hu and the latter for the machining of smaller pa such as brackets, counterweights, and cylind Functions located at Nishinomiya included bl machining and propeller assembly.

Productive activity at these dispersed sites t place only during the last 2 months of war, was brought to a halt prematurely at the Nishi miya brewery because many of the buildings w destroyed in a raid on the Nishinomiya urban a on 6 August 1945.

Because of the hurried last-minute nature of dispersal program, ineffective installation of c ine tools, and the lack of preparation at the t themselves, the Sakurajima plant suffered a gre production loss due to dispersal than did any o Sumitomo propeller plant. Taking the May production as 100 percent, it was estimated in June production had dropped to 30 percent that by August 1945 output totalled only 10 cent of the May figure.

INTELLIGENCE CHECK

The Military Intelligence Service G-2, Department, correctly assessed the Sakura plant as producing propellers for both Army Navy aircraft but erred with regard to the t produced. It was known by MIS G-2 and the Target Group that the plant occupied a sectic the extensive Sumitomo facilities in the Sal jima area but prisoner of war interrogation documentary and photo intelligence were not ficient to define its exact boundaries.

No assessment was made of the producti individual Sumitomo plants. Estimates of

oto 3—Sogo Department Store, Shinsaibashi, Osaka. The workers entrance to the Sumitomo propeller plant in the basements is located behind the truck parked in the side alley. Machine tools were lowered into the basements through openings broken in the glass-brick sidewalk which formerly served as a light shaft. The main office and machine shop of the Sakurajima plant dispersed to this site in June 1945.

Photo 4—Matzuzakaya Department Store at Kawara-cho, Osaka. The Ebisu plant of the Sakurajima plant dispersed to this site in June 1945. Photo shows west front of store.

Photo 5—View of Sogo Department Store basement showing drills, miller, and stacked parts.

hoto 6—View of second basement of Sogo Department Store showing lathes and stacks of unfinished parts.

47

Photo 7—Bench milling machine tools; second basement Matsuzakaya Store, Ebisu plant.

Photo 8—Lathes in second basement, Matsuzakaya Store, Ebisu plant.

Photo 9—Lathes in basement of Matsuzakaya Store, Osaka.

Photo 10—Outer diameter grinders in basement of Matsuzakaya Store, Osaka.

Sumitomo propeller output were low due to the insufficiency of basic data and the fact that the existence of two new Sumitomo propeller plants at Tsu and Shizuoka was not known.

REFERENCE ITEMS

The following is on file with the United States Strategic Bombing Survey, Aircraft Division, Adjutant General's Office, War Department, Washington, D. C.:

REFERENCE ITEM 1—Machine tool schedules for Sakurajima plant (raids of 1 June 1945 and 24 July 1945) and dispersal shops at the Sogo and Matsuzakaya Department Stores and Nishinomiya Brewery (raid of 6 August 1945).

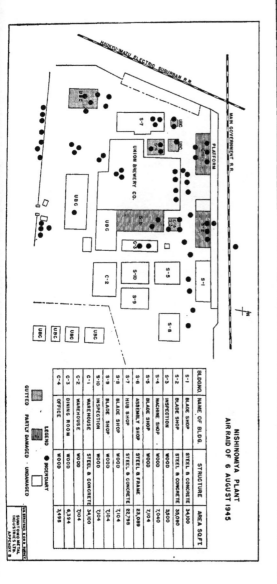

NISHINOMIYA PLANT
AIR RAID OF 6 AUGUST 1945

HANKYU-IMAZU ELECTRIC SUBURBAN R.R.
MAIN GOVERNMENT R.R.
PLATFORM
UNION BREWERY CO.

BLDG.NO.	NAME OF BLDG.	STRUCTURE	AREA SQ.FT.
S-1	BLADE SHOP	STEEL & CONCRETE	34,100
S-2	BLADE SHOP	STEEL & CONCRETE	38,080
S-3	INSPECTION	WOOD	3,500
S-4	MACHINE SHOP	WOOD	7,040
S-5	BLADE SHOP	WOOD	7,104
S-6	ASSEMBLY SHOP	STEEL & FRAME	23,089
S-7	HUB SHOP	STEEL & CONCRETE	22,798
S-8	BLADE SHOP	WOOD	7,104
S-9	BLADE SHOP	WOOD	7,104
S-10	INSPECTION	WOOD	7,104
C-1	WAREHOUSE	STEEL & CONCRETE	34,100
C-2	WAREHOUSE	WOOD	7,104
C-3	DINING ROOM	WOOD	6,364
C-4	OFFICE	WOOD	3,498

LEGEND
GUTTED   PARTLY DAMAGED   UNDAMAGED   ● INCENDIARY

U.S. STRATEGIC BOMB. SURVEY
SUMITOMO METAL
INDUSTRIES LTD.
APPENDIX B

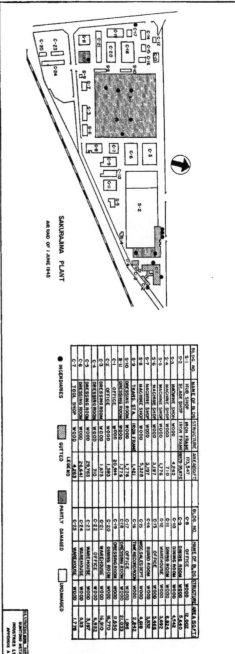

SAKURAJIMA PLANT
AIR RAID OF 1 JUNE 1945

LEGEND
● INCENDIARIES   GUTTED   PARTLY DAMAGED   UNDAMAGED

BLDG. NO.	NAME OF BLDG.	STRUCTURE	AREA SQ.FT.
S-1	HUB SHOP	IRON FRAME	173,547
S-2	BLADE SHOP	IRON FRAME	29,978-35,876
S-3	MACHINE SHOP	WOOD	4,862
S-4	MACHINE SHOP	WOOD	710
S-5	MACHINE SHOP	WOOD	1,776
S-6	MACHINE SHOP	WOOD	3,197
S-7	MACHINE SHOP	WOOD	3,197
S-8	MACHINE SHOP	WOOD	5,328
C-9	TRANS. STA.	IRON FRAME	1,481
S-10	DRESSING ROOM	WOOD	1,776
S-11	DRESSING ROOM	WOOD	1,776
C-1	OFFICE	WOOD	20,844
C-2	OFFICE	WOOD	1,593
C-3	DRESSING ROOM	WOOD	1,873
C-4	DRESSING ROOM	WOOD	710
C-5	DRESSING ROOM	WOOD	29,763
C-6	DRESSING ROOM	WOOD	26,641
C-7	TOOL SHOP	WOOD	4,263

BLDG. NO.	NAME OF BLDG.	STRUCTURE	AREA SQ.FT.
C-8	OFFICE	WOOD	12,002
C-9	DINING ROOM	WOOD	9,640
C-10	DINING ROOM	WOOD	4,542
C-11	DINING ROOM	WOOD	4,542
C-12	WAREHOUSE	WOOD	5,824
C-13	OFFICE	WOOD	5,492
C-14	OFFICE	WOOD	3,832
C-15	GUARD ROOM	WOOD	3,832
C-16	TIME RECORD ROOM	WOOD	4,618
C-17	MISC. SALES DEPT.	WOOD	2,842
C-18	DRESSING ROOM	WOOD	1,986
C-19	OFFICE	WOOD	21,033
C-20	DRESSING ROOM	WOOD	11,550
C-21	DINING ROOM	WOOD	16,770
C-22	OFFICE	WOOD	16,910
C-23	WAREHOUSE	WOOD	5,932
C-24	WAREHOUSE	WOOD	3,197
C-25	WAREHOUSE	WOOD	5,113
C-26	WAREHOUSE	WOOD	1,776

U.S. STRATEGIC BOMB. SURVEY
SUMITOMO METAL
INDUSTRIES LTD.
APPENDIX A

APPENDIX C

Dispersal From the Sakurajima Works

Name of dispersed plant	Sakurajima works	Ebisu plant	Nishinomiya plant
ition of dispersed sites:........	Second and third basements of the Sogo Department store at Shinsaibashi, Osaka; this store remained intact amidst an area devastated by raids on the Osaka urban area.	Second and third basements of the Matsuzakaya department store at Kawara Cho, Osaka; this store remained intact amidst an area devastated by raids on the Osaka urban area.	Various buildings of the Union Beer Brewery at Nishinomiya.
r area of dispersal site:........	239,948 sq. ft......................	89,372 sq. ft......................	243,107 sq. ft.
ance from original Sakurajima orks...........................	4 miles............................	34 miles...........................	8 miles.
hine tool dispersal plan:.......	131...............................	249...............................	127.
ial number of machine tools spersed:......................	131...............................	249...............................	127.
ned dispersal of employees:....	1,000.............................	1,600.............................	1,100.
ial number of employees spersed:.....................	1,019.............................	116...............................	1,076.
entage completion of dispersal le:...........................	100 percent......................	100 percent......................	90 percent.
ction of dispersal site:.........	Machining of large parts for Hamilton type propellers: bases, spiders, hubs. The main office of the Sakurajima works was transferred to this location and thus the original plant name was retained.	Machining of small parts for Hamilton type propellers: brackets, cylinders, counterweights, and sundry small parts.	Machining of blades and assembly of Hamilton type propellers. It was also planned to assemble VDM type propellers from parts supplied by the Kanzaki works.
e on which production mmenced:....................	1 July 1945.....................	17 June 1945.....................	25 July 1945.
e on which production rminated:...................	15 August 1945...................	15 August 1945...................	6 August 1945 (assembly plant destroyed in urban area raids).

51

UNITED STATES STRATEGIC BOMBING SURVEY

LIST OF REPORTS

The following is a bibliography of reports resulting from the Survey's studies of the European and Pacific wars. Certain of these reports may be purchased from the Superintendent of Documents at the Government Printing Office, Washington. D. C. Permission to examine the remaining reports may be had by writing to the Headquarters of the Survey at Gravelly Point, Washington 25, D. C.

European War
OFFICE OF THE CHAIRMAN

1 The United States Strategic Bombing Survey: Summary Report (European War)
2 The United States Strategic Bombing Survey: Over-all Report (European War)
3 The Effects of Strategic Bombing on the German War Economy

AIRCRAFT DIVISION
(By Division and Branch)
4 Aircraft Division Industry Report
5 Inspection Visits to Various Targets (Special Report)

Airframes Branch
6 Junkers Aircraft and Aero Engine Works, Dessau, Germany
7 Erla Maschinenwerke G m b H, Heiterblick, Germany
8 A T G Maschinenbau, G m b H, Leipzig (Mockau), Germany
9 Gothaer Waggonfabrik, A. G. Gotha, Germany
10 Focke Wulf Aircraft Plant, Bremen, Germany
11 Messerschmitt A G, Augsburg, Germany { Overall Report / Part A / Part B / Appendices I, II, III
12 Dornier Works, Friedrichshafen & Munich, Germany
13 Gerhard Fieseler Werke G m b H, Kassel, Germany
14 Wiener Neustaedter Flugzeugwerke, Wiener Neustade, Austria

Aero Engines Branch
15 Bussing NAG Flugmotorenwerke G m b H, Brunswick, Germany
16 Mittel-Deutsche Motorenwerke G m b H, Taucha, Germany
17 Bavarian Motorworks Inc., Eisenach & Durrerhof, Germany
18 Bayerische Motorenwerke A G (BMW) Munich, Germany
19 Henschel Flugmotorenwerke, Kassel, Germany

Light Metal Branch
20 Light Metals Industry of Germany { Part I, Aluminum / Part II, Magnesium

21 Vereinigte Deutsche Metallwerke, Hildesheim, (many
22 Metallgussgesellschaft G m b H, Leipzig, Germ
23 Aluminumwerk G m b H, Plant No. 2, Bitterf Germany
24 Gebrueder Giulini G m b H, Ludwigshafen, (many
25 Luftschiffbau Zeppelin G m b H, Friedrichsho on Bodensee, Germany
26 Wieland Werke A G, Ulm, Germany
27 Rudolph Rautenbach Leichtmetallgiessereien, lingen, Germany
28 Lippewerke Vereinigte Aluminiumwerke, A Lunen, Germany
29 Vereinigte Deutsche Metallwerke, Heddernhe Germany
30 Duerener Metallwerke A G, Duren Wittenau-Be & Waren, Germany

AREA STUDIES DIVISION
31 Area Studies Division Report
32 A Detailed Study of the Effects of Area Bomt on Hamburg
33 A Detailed Study of the Effects of Area Bomt on Wuppertal
34 A Detailed Study of the Effects of Area Bom on Dusseldorf
35 A Detailed Study of the Effects of Area Bom on Solingen
36 A Detailed Study of the Effects of Area Bom on Remscheid
37 A Detailed Study of the Effects of Area Bom on Darmstadt
38 A Detailed Study of the Effects of Area Bom on Lubeck
39 A Brief Study of the Effects of Area Bombin; Berlin, Augsburg, Bochum, Leipzig, Hagen, I mund, Oberhausen, Schweinfurt, and Bremen

CIVILIAN DEFENSE DIVISION
40 Civilian Defense Division—Final Report
41 Cologne Field Report
42 Bonn Field Report
43 Hanover Field Report
44 Hamburg Field Report—Vol. I, Text; Vol. II, hibits
45 Bad Oldesloe Field Report
46 Augsburg Field Report
47 Reception Areas in Bavaria, Germany

EQUIPMENT DIVISION
Electrical Branch
48 German Electrical Equipment Industry Repor
49 Brown Boveri et Cie, Mannheim Kafertal, Geri

Effects of Bombing on Railroad Installations in Regensburg, Nurnberg and Munich Divisions
German Locomotive Industry During the War
German Military Railroad Traffic

UTILITIES DIVISION

German Electric Utilities Industry Report
1 to 10 in Vol I "Utilities Division Plant Reports"
11 to 20 in Vol II "Utilities Division Plant Reports"
21 Rheinische-Westfalische Elektrizitaetswerk A G

Pacific War

OFFICE OF THE CHAIRMAN

Summary Report (Pacific War)
Japan's Struggle to End The War
The Effects of Atomic Bombs on Hiroshima and Nagasaki

CIVILIAN STUDIES

Civilian Defense Division

Field Report Covering Air Raid Protection and Allied Subjects, Tokyo, Japan
Field Report Covering Air Raid Protection and Allied Subjects, Nagasaki, Japan
Field Report Covering Air Raid Protection and Allied Subjects, Kyoto, Japan
Field Report Covering Air Raid Protection and Allied Subjects, Kobe, Japan
Field Report Covering Air Raid Protection and Allied Subjects, Osaka, Japan
Field Report Covering Air Raid Protection and Allied Subjects, Hiroshima, Japan—No. 1
Summary Report Covering Air Raid Protection and Allied Subjects in Japan
Final Report Covering Air Raid Protection and Allied Subjects in Japan

Medical Division

The Effects of Bombing on Health and Medical Services in Japan
The Effects of Atomic Bombs on Health and Medical Services in Hiroshima and Nagasaki

Morale Division

The Effects of Strategic Bombing on Japanese Morale

ECONOMIC STUDIES

Aircraft Division

The Japanese Aircraft Industry

Mitsubishi Heavy Industries, Ltd.
Corporation Report No. I
(Mitsubishi Jukogyo KK)
(Airframes & Engines)

Nakajima Aircraft Company, Ltd.
Corporation Report No. II
(Nakajima Hikoki KK)
(Airframes & Engines)

18 Kawanishi Aircraft Company
Corporation Report No. III
Kawanishi Kokuki Kabushiki Kaisha)
(Airframes)

19 Kawasaki Aircraft Industries Company, Inc.
Corporation Report No. IV
(Kawasaki Kokuki Kogyo Kabushiki Kaisha)
(Airframes & Engines)

20 Aichi Aircraft Company
Corporation Report No. V
(Aichi Kokuki KK)
(Airframes & Engines)

21 Sumitomo Metal Industries, Propeller Division
Corporation Report No. VI
(Sumitomo Kinzoku Kogyo KK, Puropera Seizosho)
(Propellers)

22 Hitachi Aircraft Company
Corporation Report No. VII
(Hitachi Kokuki KK)
(Airframes & Engines)

23 Japan International Air Industries, Ltd.
Corporation Report No. VIII
(Nippon Kokusai Koku Kogyo KK)
(Airframes)

24 Japan Musical Instrument Manufacturing Company
Corporation Report No. IX
(Nippon Gakki Seizo KK)
(Propellers)

25 Tachikawa Aircraft Company
Corporation Report No. X
(Tachikawa Hikoki KK)
(Airframes)

26 Fuji Airplane Company
Corporation Report No. XI
(Fuji Hikoki KK)
(Airframes)

27 Showa Airplane Company
Corporation Report No. XII
(Showa Hikoki Kogyo KK)
(Airframes)

28 Ishikawajima Aircraft Industries Company, Ltd.
Corporation Report No. XIII
(Ishikawajima Koku Kogyo Kabushiki Kaisha)
(Engines)

29 Nippon Airplane Company
Corporation Report No. XIV
(Nippon Hikoki KK)
(Airframes)

30 Kyushu Airplane Company
Corporation Report No. XV
(Kyushu Hikoki KK)
(Airframes)

Report of Ships Bombardment Survey Party (Enclosure J), Comments and Data on Accuracy of Firing

Reports of Ships Bombardment Survey Party (Enclosure K), Effects of Surface Bombardments on Japanese War Potential

Physical Damage Division

Effect of the Incendiary Bomb Attacks on Japan (a Report on Eight Cities)

The Effects of the Ten Thousand Pound Bomb on Japanese Targets (a Report on Nine Incidents)

Effects of the Atomic Bomb on Hiroshima, Japan

Effects of the Atomic Bomb on Nagasaki, Japan

Effects of the Four Thousand Pound Bomb on Japanese Targets (a Report on Five Incidents)

Effects of Two Thousand, One Thousand, and Five Hundred Pound Bombs on Japanese Targets (a Report on Eight Incidents)

A Report on Physical Damage in Japan (Summary Report)

G-2 Division

Japanese Military and Naval Intelligence

Evaluation of Photographic Intelligence in the Japanese Homeland, Part I, *Comprehensive Report*

99 Evaluation of Photographic Intelligence in the Japanese Homeland, Part II, *Airfields*

100 Evaluation of Photographic Intelligence in the Japanese Homeland, Part III, *Computed Bomb Plotting*

101 Evaluation of Photographic Intelligence in the Japanese Homeland, Part IV, *Urban Area Analysis*

102 Evaluation of Photographic Intelligence in the Japanese Homeland, Part V, *Camouflage*

103 Evaluation of Photographic Intelligence in the Japanese Homeland, Part VI, *Shipping*

104 Evaluation of Photographic Intelligence in the Japanese Homeland, Part VII, *Electronics*

105 Evaluation of Photographic Intelligence in the Japanese Homeland, Part VIII, *Beach Intelligence*

106 Evaluation of Photographic Intelligence in the Japanese Homeland, Part IX, *Artillery*

107 Evaluation of Photographic Intelligence in the Japanese Homeland, Part X, *Roads and Railroads*

108 Evaluation of Photographic Intelligence in the Japanese Homeland, Part XI, *Industrial Analysis*

☆ U. S. GOVERNMENT PRINTING OFFICE: 1946—704697